Otsego Lodge No. 138, F. & A. M.
Cooperstown, New York

Otsego Lodge No. 138, F. & A. M. Cooperstown, New York

A Collection of Historical Miscellanea
1795-2007

Published in Honor of
the Bicentennial of the Incorporation of
the Village of Cooperstown

Compiled with Commentary
by Richard Vang

Square Circle Press

Otsego Lodge No. 138, F. & A. M., Cooperstown, New York:
A Collection of Historical Miscellanea, 1795-2007

©2007, Otsego Lodge No. 138 , F. & A. M.

Published by
Square Circle Press LLC
137 Ketcham Road
Voorheesville, NY 12186
(518) 432-6657
www.squarecirclepress.com

All rights reserved. No part of this publication may be reproduced or transmitted in any form or by any means, electronic or mechanical, including photocopying, recording, taping, or any other information retrieval system, without permission in writing from the publisher.

ISBN 13: 978-0-9789066-2-7
ISBN 10: 0-9789066-2-4

Library of Congress Control Number: 2007906572

Printed and bound in the United State of America.

Contents

Preface	vii
Illustrations	viii
Masonic Terms and Abbreviations	ix
Introduction: Otsego Lodge Historiography	1
Van Horne's Centennial History (1896) (facsimile reprint)	5
Van Horne's Updated History (1906) (facsimile reprint)	39
Dunn's Bicentennial History (1995) (facsimile reprint)	53
History of Otsego Lodge Buildings	67
Charters of Otsego Lodge	77
Masters of Otsego Lodge	81
Noteworthy Members of Otsego Lodge	85
Sources	89

Preface

This small book on the history of Freemasonry in Cooperstown was quickly compiled in an attempt to provide a commemorative publication for the celebration surrounding the bicentennial anniversary of the village's incorporation. As a historical contribution, the intent of this volume is to provide a collection of previously published historical writings, present a little statistical data on Otsego Lodge, and give the non-Masonic public an overview of the story of this important village organization. As this book is geared more toward that audience, Masons may find some of the information obvious and elementary.

With Freemasonry it is always difficult to gauge just how much the public knows or doesn't know about the subject. Many see Freemasonry as a secret society, or at the very least, an organization that has secrets. Both interpretations are untrue. While Masonic meetings, like those of many other private organizations, are usually open only to members, its members are usually very publicly-involved citizens. Upon occasion public events are even held in a lodge room. Masonic ritual, sensationalized by cable television and modern novels and considered hokey, antiquated or downright sinister by others, is meaningful to its members and is what sets it apart from all other organizations.

Apart from what I have written and included myself, I am unsure if any of the previous histories presented here have been made public before or if they were published only for the benefit of the lodge members. I do know that there are life-long residents of the village who claim to know nothing about their local Freemasons and or to never have seen the inside of the lodge rooms. After reading this book, I hope that Cooperstown's residents will feel that they know this institution and will recognize that it has been visible, all along, its members contributing to their daily life as friends, neighbors and colleagues.

Due to its hasty publication, this book may raise more questions than it answers, as some legends, facts and events remain to be more fully explored. Perhaps this will encourage other local historians to conduct their own research and fill out the story. Cooperstonians love their history, and I hope this will sate their thirst for historical knowledge until a full-scale history can be written and published in 2011, the 215th anniversary of Otsego Lodge.

Until then,

Richard Vang
Past Master, Lodge Historian
September 2007
Knox, New York

Illustrations

Manuscript of written history from 1862   3

Masonic chart from the Otsego Lodge collections   4

Albert T. Van Horne   6

Cornerstone and copper plate from original lodge building   38

Alton G. Dunn, Jr.   54

The Smithy building annex   65

Masonic symbols in the stonework of The Smithy annex   66

Original Otsego Lodge Masonic Hall   75

The Phinney Block and the Bunyan Block   76

Elihu Phinney   80

Portraits of noteworthy members of Otsego Lodge are inserted by their biographies beginning on page 86.

Masonic Terms and Abbreviations

Like any subculture of society, Freemasonry employs its own vocabulary, abbreviations and dates. While the use of this specialized lingo has been mostly avoided in the new writings and commentaries, the facsimiles of the previous histories contain many terms particular to Masonry. These are briefly explained here for the benefit of readers who are not Freemasons.

Within the Grand Lodge of the State of New York there are basically four terms or titles used to distinguish the "rank" of an individual Mason. The term "member" or "brother" is used to identify a single Mason. (The plural forms of these terms are obvious in their usage.)

The title of respect "Worshipful" refers to a Mason who has served as the Master of a lodge. The titles "Very Worshipful" and "Right Worshipful" refer to a Mason who has served the Grand Lodge in some capacity, the title "Most Worshipful" being reserved for Grand Masters or to the organization of the Grand Lodge itself. Sometimes these titles are abbreviated as "Br.", "Bro.", "W", "VW", "RW" or "MW", and are often followed by a symbolic punctuation (M∴W∴). This symbol can be used most anywhere as a way to abbreviate any Masonic term.

The term "lodge" is used in various forms and can refer to either a formally organized group of Masons, such as Otsego Lodge, or to the building where that entity holds its meetings. Sometimes it even refers to the meeting itself. Hopefully these distinctions are obvious when read in context.

The Masonic dating system is based upon the chronology of 17th-century Anglican Archbishop James Ussher, who determined his cosmological dates while the modern Masonic order was still organizing itself. The Masonic year is calculated by simply adding 4,000 years to the current year. Freemasons obviously do not believe that their organization dates back to the beginning of the world, but that the symbolic principles upon which Masonry is based were born with Creation. Thus, our current Western calendar year would be 6007 in the "Year of Light" (Anno Lucis, or A∴L∴) on the Masonic calendar.

Introduction: Otsego Lodge Historiography

As a community institution, Otsego Lodge has existed since before William Cooper's Town became an actual incorporated village in 1807. Its members have been a part of the very fabric of village life since the lodge was first chartered in 1795. Any history of Cooperstown would inevitably include the names of lodge members as community leaders.

With such a lengthy past, the story of Otsego Lodge as a local institution is often tedious and sometimes vague, but always complex. Each meeting of a Masonic lodge is meticulously recorded in their minute book, and the minutes of the previous meeting are read and approved at either the end of the current meeting or at the beginning of the next meeting. Besides the reading of the minutes, once a lodge secretary puts pen to paper (or rather, fingers to keyboard), the minutes all but disappear. The lodge members rarely see them, even though all are allowed to do so. The public almost never sees them, as Masonic law forbids minute books to leave a currently operating Masonic lodge building and the archives are opened only to researchers by special request.

Otsego Lodge, like many lodges in New York State, includes in its list of officers an Historian who is appointed by the Master of the lodge. The duties of the office are to compile an annual record of the activities of the lodge. Since 1895, this lodge has been fortunate to have been served by some able historians over the years who have kept, with few exceptions, at least a statistical digest of each year since the office was instituted.

This being said, writing a history of Otsego Lodge is understandably a vast undertaking. Besides the minute books, there are stacks of documents related to the operation of the lodge, artifacts that bear some unique story, random pieces of paper, greeting cards, scrapbooks and undocumented photographs. Otsego Lodge has been fortunate over the centuries not to have lost any records due to fire, flood or other calamity. But to the lodge historian, this good fortune presents a truly daunting task. One may wonder then why anyone would want this job. It is certainly not for the pay.

As for myself, I suppose it is simply the joy of research and the love of old things. In the case of Otsego Lodge, there is a palpable continuity of more than 200 years that is uncommon in social organizations in America. When I can hold a piece of parchment written in 1795 by the hand of Elihu Phinney and read his desire to form a lodge, I can only look upon it with reverence for him and his efforts and all of those caretakers in between. As any researcher knows, it can be a sublime experience. When Alton G. Dunn, Jr. asked me to take over for him as Historian, I was excited—and a little overwhelmed.

During my tenure I have done some historical writings on the lodge, but mainly I have focused on organizing what records we have and displaying important artifacts. My research has barely begun, and I have only been able to stand on the shoulders of those historians who have come and gone before me. I guess my reverence and love for Otsego Lodge is evident in the fact that while I live near Albany, I still make the long drive west to be a part of it.

There have been at least six attempts at a written history of Otsego Lodge that I am aware of. The three "published" versions are reproduced in this book: 1) Van Horne's centennial history, 2) his 1906 update, and 3) Dunn's bicentennial pamphlet. The program for the sesquicentennial anniversary banquet in 1945 documents a lodge history being delivered by historian Frank B. Carpenter. A brief, one-page history is included in the program for dinner guests, written by previous historian Rowan D. Spraker, Sr. Carpenter's history is assumed to have once existed in some type of paper or manuscript, but has not been located. Two other handwritten manuscripts have been kept in our archives that were obviously unfinished histories, and about which we currently know nothing.

The earlier manuscript covers the time from the lodge's founding up to 1862. It consists of 88 pages in a stitched notebook format. A photo appears on the next page, but a facsimile was not reproduced here because of its poor condition. There is no name inscribed upon it, but the Secretary at that time was Robert C. Flack, and the Corresponding Secretary was E. B. Crandall. A handwriting match has not been conducted against the minute books for this pair of candidates. I do not believe it is Van Horne's draft manuscript, because he did not join until 1880 and the handwriting does not match examples of his. I do believe, however, that he used it as a source for his centennial history because the wording is almost identical. Due to the haste with which this current volume was put together, a transcription was impossible and will have to await further research.

The later manuscript consists of only five loose handwritten pages and one additional page of notes. Once again the pages bear no signature. Apart from a brief narrative of lodge origins, it consists primarily of a list of lodge Masters from 1796 through 1879, the latter date, or perhaps 1880, being the likely date it was compiled. Although, again, the handwriting does not match Van Horne's, I suppose it is possible that since he joined the lodge in 1880, he may have acted upon a natural inclination for scholarship and begun a history in just his first year. (New members are often zealous in that way, and handwriting does change over decades.) However, without further research and knowing more about the personal biography of Van Horne, it is impossible to know at this time who the author was.

It has only been in the past two decades that academic scholars have begun to treat Freemasonry as a valid subject for research and as a valuable source of primary materials. Apart from occasional mentions, brief narratives in local histories and rare graduate theses, the only treatments of Otsego Lodge in publications of a national scale are those in Dr. Alan Taylor's Pulitzer Prize-winning book, <u>William Cooper's Town: Power and Persuasion on the Frontier of the Early American Republic</u>, and in the more recent <u>A Strasbourger in America: John Frederick Ernst, Minister of the Gospel, Lutheran Denomination (1748-1805)</u>, by Dr. Edith von Zemenszky.

Dr. von Zemenszky contacted me to help her with research on Rev. Ernst's Masonic membership. She had read Dr. Taylor's information about the Reverend's involvement with the lodge, and wondered if there was anything more in the lodge minutes about the transient minister's original membership or his disputes with fellow Masons.

After cross-referencing Taylor's footnotes against the lodge minutes, I believe that some of his citations are incorrect or non-existent. I think he may have misinterpreted the information in the minute books and portrayed the events surrounding Ernst inaccurately. He also made some sweeping generalizations about Freemasonry that I think are misleading. I don't know the reason for this, but I believe it is because he didn't really understand the inner workings of Freemasonry. I don't know if he was given direct access to the lodge archives or if the information was given to him inaccurately. I haven't discussed this with Dr. Taylor and the previous Historian is no longer living, so I remain puzzled. I hope my explanations of Freemasonry in general have helped Dr. von Zemenszky make more sense of the Ernst matter, which I look forward to reading. It goes without saying that I welcome the chance to compare research notes with Dr. Taylor.

The 1862 history manuscript, author unknown.

A Masonic chart from the Otsego Lodge collections.
(A description can be found on page 30.)

Van Horne's Centennial History (1896)

Albert T. Van Horne was initiated into Otsego Lodge in 1880 and served as Master three times (1887, 1888, 1896). He was elected to the office of Secretary for the years preceding the lodge's centennial, 1890-1895. He was appointed a committee member for the anniversary celebration and presumably his intimacy with the lodge minutes was the reason a centennial history became his to write. The book mentions his history being read (by someone else) during the centennial banquet on August 14, 1895. It is assumed that a manuscript version was read and the information about the celebration was added to that for final publication. The members must have felt so strongly about his efforts that they elected him Master the following year.

The centennial history was a quality publication for its day, as far as paper bound books are concerned. It measures 5.75 x 8 inches in size, with a light blue paper cover set in black type. The 118 pages are thread-sewn and printed on a heavy, textured stock. The volume bears the imprint of "S. M. SHAW & CO., PRINTERS, COOPERSTOWN, N. Y." on the fourth page (the reverse of the title page). A dedication appears on the fifth page:

> *To the faithful of the Craft, with whom I have had the most pleasant associations, and by whose courtesy I have received the highest honors at their command, this volume is fra= ternally inscribed.*

The cover and title page show that the book contained much more than what is reproduced here in this current volume. The additional information will be considered in the forthcoming full history in 2011. The following is a list of the full contents of Van Horne's book, including the actual chapter titles and relevant short commentary (in parentheses).

- Copy of Original Charter. (Actually just the text, not an image of the original document. This is briefly discussed, on page 77.)
- History of Otsego Lodge, F. & A. M. (Reproduced here in full, without the original page numbers to avoid confusion with page numbers in this current volume.)
- Officers of Otsego Lodge, No. 40-41-138. (These tables include the entire set of each year's officers, as do the other lists below.)
- Members of Otsego Lodge, No. 40-41-138. (Listed by year of lodge initiation or affiliation.)
- History of Otsego Mark Masters' Lodge, No. 5. (Mark Master lodges were the fraternal ancestor of Royal Arch Masonry.)
- Officers of Otsego Mark Lodge No. 5, and date of their election.
- Members of Otsego Mark Lodge Number 5.

- History of Otsego Chapter, No. 26, Royal Arch Masons. (Royal Arch Masonry is a York Rite concordant body operating within the greater Masonic family.)
- Officers of Otsego Chapter No. 26, and date of their election.
- Members of Otsego Chapter, No. 26, R. A. M.
- History of Otsego Council, No. 45, Royal and Select Masters. (The Council is an organization within York Rite Masonry.)
- Officers of Otsego Council, No. 45, R. & S. M.
- Members of Otsego Council, No. 45, R. & S. M.
- IN MEMORIAM. (Chapter title page bordered in black, followed by introductory text and a list of deceased members. Van Horne states that is an incomplete list, and suggests that he listed the names of members who distinguished themselves within the lodge.)

Van Horne's book contains some typographical errors (some of which he corrected in the 1906 updated version). Some comments, corrections and notes have been inserted below some facsimile pages of the book. They are intended as extended information and a correction where considered necessary.

The most glaring error appears on the title page of the book (reproduced in this volume) which reads, "Centennial History of Freemasonary". The correct terminology, of course, is "Freemasonry," without the second "a". Although now "masonry" is used for both meanings, "masonary" is an older usage that usually relates to the operative skill of stonework or bricklaying. I know of no other instance in which the title page spelling is used to name the organization. This is undoubtedly the fault of the typesetter, as Van Horne uses the proper term throughout the book. No doubt he took an incredible amount of good-natured ribbing from his fellow Masons, because the title page of his 1906 update bears the accepted spelling.

Fraternally Yours,

Albert T. Van Horne

HISTORY

-:- OF -:-

OTSEGO LODGE

No. 138, F. & A. M. And

Mark Lodge,
Chapter, and Council.

COOPERSTOWN, N. Y.

CENTENNIAL

History :: Freemasonary

EMBRACING

Otsego Lodge, No. 138, F. & A. M.
Otsego Mark Lodge, No. 5.
Otsego Chapter, No. 26, R. A. M.
Otsego Council, No. 45, R. & S. M.

COOPERSTOWN, N. Y.

BY ALBERT T. VAN HORNE.

March 1st, 1896.

History of Otsego Lodge, F. & A. M.
Cooperstown, Otsego Co., N. Y.

PREVIOUS to April, 1795, the dispersed Brethren who had removed into the county of Otsego associated themselves together, and Bro's Elihu Phinney, Rowland Cotton, James Fitch, B. Gilbert, R. Bartlett and R. Edwards, petitioned for a charter to erect a Lodge at Cooperstown, in said county.

Bro. Peter W. Yates, a lawyer in Albany, interested himself in their behalf, and seconded by his exertions, a Warrant was granted by the "Grand Lodge of the State of New York, established under the auspices of Prince Edwin, of the city of York, in Great Britain, in the year of Masonry, A. L. 4926."

The Warrant, sealed and signed by M. W. Robert R. Livingston, Grand Master; R. W. Jacob Morton, Deputy Grand Master; R. W. James Scott, Senior Grand Warden; R. W. De Witt Glinton, Junior Grand Warden, and R. W. John Abrams, Grand Sec'y, was dated Aug. 14th, A. L. 5795, and established a Lodge to be known as "Otsego Lodge No. 40," naming as the first Officers: Bro. Elihu Phinney, W. M.; Bro. Rowland Cotton, S. W.; and Bro. James Fitch, J. W.

About Sept. 1st, 1795, a dispensation was granted to install the Officers, and in due time the Officers named in the Warrant proceeded to Albany, and were duly installed in the stations therein named.

The cost of the Warrant was £12.

Jewels and Platform were procured by Bro. Peter W. Yates.

The first meeting was held at the house of Wor. Bro. E. Phinney, March 1st, 1796, who having convened the Brethren, appointed the following Officers, in addition to those already installed: Bro's B. Gilbert, Treasurer; R. Bartlett, Sec'y; R.

Par. 3: Obviously Dewitt Clinton, not "Glinton" was the Junior Grand Warden.

Edwards, S. D.; L. Edson, J. D.; S. Ingalls, Sen. Steward; Levi Collar, Junior Steward, and E. Eaton, Tyler.

Present also, Bro's Gott, Tanner, Draper and Parker.

Being thus organized, the Lodge was formally opened and proceeded to business.

At this meeting Bro. Edwards proposed the names of Elijah Holt, Esq., and Thomas Whitaker; Bro. Gott the names of Timothy Morse and Capt. Wm. Abbott, and Bro. Cotton the name of Anselm Williams, as candidates for initiation.

At an "Extra Lodge" held on the same day, Elijah Holt, Esq., was balloted for and accepted, and the candidate was duly initiated.

Accounts of the Lodge were kept in pounds, shillings and pence.

It was unanimously resolved that "this Lodge shall be held on the first Tuesday of each month," at 3 o'clock P. M. This time of meeting was continued until January, 1808, when it was changed to the "Tuesday preceding the full moon, at 3 o'clock P. M."

After 1812 meetings were held at a later hour. May 13, 1862, by resolution of the Lodge, the time was changed from Tuesday to Saturday evenings, and Feb. 18th, 1868, the By-Laws were amended to hold meetings on the first and third Tuesdays of each month, excepting June, July and August, which should have but one meeting,—on the first Tuesday thereof.

October 4th, 1796, it was voted "that Bro. Worshipful Elihu Phinney provide a Bible for the use of the Lodge, to the amount of seventeen dollars." This Bible, bearing date of 1791, has since been, and still remains, in use by the Lodge.

Beginning with Dec. 27th, 1796, it was the custom of the Lodge for many years to celebrate the Festivals of St. John the Evangelist and St. John the Baptist, usually by a sermon at "Academy Hall," or one of the village churches, followed by a dinner and toasts, at the Lodge Room. Many of these sermons were published for the benefit of the Craft, and several copies are still in the Archives of the Lodge.

On the 7th of March, 1797, it was resolved "to build a Ma-

Par. 9: The 1791 Phinney bible is still in their possession but is no longer used by the lodge because of its deteriorated condition.

sonic Hall the ensuing season, not to exceed the expense of £300."

Bro's T. Tanner, Sen., Phinney, Edwards, Gilbert and Dewey were appointed a committee "vested with discretionary powers in erecting said building, not exceeding said sum of £300." Each brother who would contribute was to "be allowed seven per cent interest until refunded."

May 2d, 1797, the committee reported that they had contracted with Bro's Sprague, Whipple and Kellogg, to "build a Masonic Hall in Cooperstown for £300," the Bond, (still retained by the Lodge), bearing that date, providing that "£100 was to be paid on raising the frame, £100 on the enclosing and glazing the same, and £100 on the completion thereof, provided that said work be approved by Tho's Tanner, Timothy Barnes and Elihu Phinney," which report was agreed to by the Lodge, and a committee appointed to select a lot on "Front street."

A lot was selected on the corner of Front and West streets (now Lake and Pioneer), and the Building Committee proceeded to erect the Hall, the frame of which was raised June 24th, 1797, with appropriate ceremonies, an Oration being delivered by Bro. Gilbert.

The corner stone was of cut limestone, bearing on the face the inscription, "A. L. 5797." A copper plate 10x5½x⅛ inches was set in the top of the stone on which was inscribed in Latin:

    ANNO LUCIS VMDCCXCVII DIE JUNII XXIV
    HÆC AULA ERECTA FUIT, A MEMBRIS
OTSEGO SOCIETY OF LATIMORUM SOCIETATIS E. P. M.
    ET DEDICATI USUI FILIORUM LUCIS.
    NON NOBIS SOLUM NATI SUMUS
    SED PARTIM PATRIÆ PARTIM AMICIS.

The translation is about as follows:

"On the 24th day of June, in the year of Light 5797, this Hall was erected by the Otsego Society of Latimorus, E. P. M., and was dedicated to the use of the Brethren of Light."

"We're born and live not to ourselves alone;
But equally for country and friends of every home."

Par. 5: For an analysis of the copper plate, its accurate engraving and an alternative translation, see page 68. A photo appears on page 38.

An explanation of the use of the term E. P. M. may be that, until a visit of the Grand Lecturer in February, 1858, the Lodge was always opened on the Entered Apprentice Degree. Hence it was often styled a "Lodge of Entered Apprentice Masons."

Previous to the sale of the premises in 1886, the stone was removed and placed in a glass case on a pedestal in the Lodge Room.

The Hall was completed, and dedicated Dec. 28, 1797, on which occasion a sermon was delivered by Bro. Ernst. A resolution of the Lodge that "no woman be allowed to dine with the Masons on the occasion," was afterward rescinded, and "the wives of Masons were invited to the festival."

Wor. Bro. Phinney composed the following song, which was sung at the dedication by Bro's Grant, Eaton and Ripley, Mrs. Kellogg, Mrs. Huntington, Miss Ernst, Miss Walker and Miss Whipple.

DEDICATION SONG.

TUNE—*"Indulgent Parents."*

Come all you Masons Free,
  Come lend your aid
To dedicate this Hall
  Which we have made.
We'll dedicate the same
To honor and to fame,
In our Grand Master's name;
  We're Masons Free!

We'll consecrate the same
  To Masonry;
And show the scoffing world
  That we are Free.
True friendship here we find
Joined to a noble mind,
While we are here combined;
  We're Masons Free!

The Corn, the Wine, the Oil,
  We here bestow,

Will Masons' pains beguile
   And soothe their woe.
True friendship here we trace
In each Freemason's face,
While we do each embrace;
     We're Masons Free!

When we shall leave this ground
   To walk the Square,
Sweet music then shall sound
   To charm the ear.
In Mystic order grand,
A Brother in each hand
Moves the fraternal band,
     Like Masons Free!

We boast an ancient state,
   Our pedigree
From Solomon the Great,
   A Mason Free.
He did the Temple rear
On Mount Moriah's square;
His workmen rallied there,
     All Masons Free!

The building he did raise
   Of stone made square,
And fitted for the place
   Ere they came there.
With Level, Plumb and Square
The work they did prepare;
No discord entered there
     'Mongst Masons Free!

From Lebanon's proud mount
   The timber came;
The stone, from quaries of
   Zarethodan.
No hammer's piercing sound
Their order did confound

> On Mount Moriah's ground,
> By Masons Free!
>
> Our glorious Architect
> We will adore;
> That he will us direct
> We will implore,
> Till fitted for that place,
> Where human work shall cease,
> Where we shall dwell in peace
> Like Masons Free!

The original MS. was recently presented to the Lodge by a grandson of Wor. Bro. Phinney, who bears his name.

By resolution, the lower rooms of the Hall were rented to Rev. Benj. Wright for one year, "he paying $10.50 and provide firewood and candles whenever the Lodge meets."

In 1813 the rent was raised to $20 per annum, in 1817 to $30, and in 1829 it was lowered to $25; then for several years only sufficient rent was required to pay the taxes and insurance.

June 5th, 1798, "Judge William Cooper having presented to this Lodge a deed of the land whereon the Hall now stands," it was "Resolved, That Bro's Phinney and Edwards be a committee to wait on him, and assure him of the gratitude and many obligations which the members of this Lodge feel toward him for the generous donation this day conferred on them."

February 22d, 1800, an oration was delivered by Bro. Parsons, in memory of "Our Illustrious Brother, George Washington."

In 1800 the Lodge was visited by the Grand Master of the Grand Lodge of New Jersey, as shown by the following extract from the minutes of July 1st, 1800:

"Resolved, unanimously, That Bro's Elihu Phinney, Richard F. Cooper and Richard Edwards be a committee to wait on the Right Worshipful Brother Joseph Bloomfield, Grand Master of the State of New Jersey, and present him with a respectful address from the Lodge."

"*Right Worshipful Brother:*

Permit the members of Otsego Lodge, through their committee, to express to you their grateful sense of the honor conferred on them by a visit from a brother so eminently distinguished in the Masonic Calendar as yourself, and to reciprocate with you the pleasure resulting from a diffusion of the sublime principles of Masonry in a district which a short time since was a wilderness.

That the genial influence of Masonry may continue to harmonize the bosoms of the fraternity, inspire the glow of benevolence and charity, and promote the fidelity of mankind to time immemorial, and that you, sir, as a Brother and a citizen, may long remain the pride and ornament of the Craft, and have a safe return to the bosom of your native State, over the Lodges of which you have the honor to preside, is the fervent wish, Right Worshipful Brother, of your respectful and affectionate brethren, ELIHU PHINNEY, RICHARD F. COOPER, RICHARD EDWARDS, } *Com.*

Cooperstown, July 4, 1800."

COOPERSTOWN, July 5, A. L. 5800.

"I acknowledge, dear Brethren, with great sensibility the reception this evening of your Address and Resolutions of the Worshipful 'The Otsego Lodge.'

For this marked attention and your affectionate good wishes you will be pleased to accept my thankful acknowledgment, and present to your Lodge the assurance of my most profound respect.

The diffusion of Masonry among the first settlers of this new country, however desirous, has made a more rapid progress than could have been expected. I learn with great pleasure it has enlightened the inhabitants in the neighborhood of this beautiful Lake, for which your Lodge bears its name. That 'The Otsego Lodge' may receive the protection and blessing of our Great Master Builder, extend the great and good object of its benevolent institutions, and that its worthy Brethren may increase with the improvements of the country, is the most fervent prayer of Your affectionate Brother,

JOSEPH BLOOMFIELD,
G. M. of M., New Jersey.

To Elihu Phinney, Richard F. Cooper, Richard Edwards, Committee for Otsego Lodge."

For many years, when Brethren were absent from several successive communications, they were summoned to attend a "Stated Meeting" and "show cause for their non-attendance."

Charges were preferred for unmasonic conduct, on very slight provocation, and personal differences were frequently settled by committees from the Lodge.

October, 1805, a petition was presented by the Brethren of Richfield, asking consent to establish a Lodge at that place, which was "laid on the table," and the records do not show any further action.

January 7th, 1806, in answer to a petition, it was resolved to recommend a Charter for a Lodge at Cherry Valley, provided that the Officers named met the approval of the members, and at the following meeting the Officers were named by this Lodge and recommended.

October 1st, 1816, this Lodge again voted to sign a petition to the Grand Lodge for a charter for Cherry Valley Lodge.

May 10th, 1808, a resolution was passed recommending to the Grand Lodge the granting of a Dispensation or Charter for a Lodge at Butternuts, Otsego county, to be known as "Butternuts Lodge."

March, 1812, a petition from the Brethren at Milford for a new Lodge at that place was refused; same presented again June 20th, 1815, and refused by a vote of eighteen to fourteen; presented again March 26th, 1826, and a petition to the Grand Lodge was approved.

A petition for consent to establish a Lodge at Oaksville was presented Dec. 16th, 1823, and again April 13th, 1824, both of which this Lodge refused to recommend, and Nov. 22d, 1825, a petition was presented for consent to remove Otsego Lodge to Oaksville.

January 13th, 1824, the Lodge officially recommended to the Grand Lodge the granting of a Warrant for a Lodge in the town of Middlefield.

That this Lodge was established is evident from the fact

that a member of this Lodge, in 1888, states that he has seen records of an extinct Lodge that was held in Clarksville,—now known as Middlefield.

In July, 1808, the Grand Lodge was asked to assist Bro. James Angel, in consequence of loss sustained by fire. During the same year a member was expelled for unmasonic conduct, and notice of the same was ordered "inserted in the publick news papers."

Consent was given to Otsego Chapter, March 13, 1809, to make such repairs to the Lodge Room, garret and one closet, at their own expense, as they deemed proper, and to occupy the same provided "that it did not interfere with the working days of Otsego Lodge, or Otsego Mark Masters' Lodge."

Refreshments were served at the meetings, consisting of crackers, cheese and gin, the same being provided by the stewards, who were reimbursed by the Lodge on presentation of bills.

In June, 1819, the Lodge No. was changed from 40 to 41, as shown by the following endorsement on the back of the original Warrant:

"In Grand Lodge of the State of New York, June 4, 1819.

Pursuant to the numerical arrangement submitted by the Grand Secretary, it was ordered that Otsego Lodge, held at Cooperstown, hitherto known as No. 40, be hereafter styled No. 41.

Proceedings of the Grand Lodge, 1819. Page 40."

Charles Thurston was the first candidate initiated after the Lodge No. was changed, who remained one of the faithful few during the dark days of Masonry, and a regular attendant of the Lodge until prevented by age and infirmities, dying at the age of 90 years, in December, 1870.

During October and November, 1827, "an honorary Degree appertaining to the Master's Lodge, established by the Grand Lodge, called the 'Check Degree,'" was conferred on sixteen members by Bro. E. B. Morehouse.

Nov. 27th, 1827, measures were taken by the Treasurer, authorized by the Lodge, by which the Lodge was incorporated

---

Par. 3: Royal Arch Masonry is a "concordant body" of Freemasonry which exemplifies a system of expanded degrees and teachings related to the rituals of "symbolic" or "blue lodge" Masonry, of which Otsego Lodge is an example. The Mark Masters' Lodge was a precursor that was subsumed into the local Royal Arch Chapter in 1809.

under an "Act of the Legislature of 1825," which vested in it the authority to own and hold real estate, and an insurance was placed on the property, the value of the Hall and lot being fixed at a sum not exceeding one thousand dollars.

In 1845 the Hall was rented to the Independent Order of Rechabites, for two years, reserving its use for the Lodge when wanted.

During the Anti-Masonic excitement which prevailed so extensively, especially in the western part of the State, it was deemed advisable to hold no meetings of the Lodge but such as were necessary to save the real estate, elect officers, etc. Thus from 1828 to 1846, with but few exceptions, only one meeting was held each year, viz.: for the election and installation of Officers, and to appoint a committee to care for the Hall and rent. From March, 1827, to September, 1846, no work was done, the first candidate being Mr. Edwin Pier.

Rt. Wor. Henry Clark, Grand Visitor, visited the Lodge in 1830, and received $6.50 "in full for dues to date." No further visits were made, and no notice of or call for dues was received by the Lodge. March 13th, 1832, a motion was made to sell the Hall, which was lost.

It was then resolved that the Treasurer be authorized "to subscribe all surplus funds in his hands toward the building of a Universalist Meeting House in this village," $56 being thus subscribed.

A resolution was passed December 16th, 1834, to "convey by quit claim deed to Horace Baldwin two feet in front and rear of the east side of the lot now owned by the Lodge, for $35, it being understood that said Baldwin is forever to keep the line fence in good repair, and that said conveyance be made at the expense of said Baldwin."

The strong anti-Masonic excitement produced in many an apathy on the subject, the tide of emigration which swept over the country took away the young and enterprising, so that in the fall of 1846, within the radius of three miles, only *nine* members belonging to this Lodge could be found, including

---

Par. 1: The "Act of the Legislature" is curious because the lodge obviously already owned property. Further investigation is necessary.

Par. 5: The subscription to the Universalist Meeting House is also strange. Unless the lodge was solicited as part of a larger group of subscribers within the village, it would be atypical of them to contribute solely to a specific religious denomination. But given the environment of the times, they may have been pressured or coerced into the large donation.

some whose infirmities were such as to prevent their attendance.

During the winter of 1847, no work having been done for many years, the elections of the Lodge having been regularly held, the members of the Lodge supposing they were still a regularly constituted Lodge, having power to meet and work; and thus persuaded, after due consideration, it was deemed advisable to gather up the fragments.

Thus with the attendance of a number of Masonic brethren who had moved into the village and vicinity, work was resumed and a few candidates were initiated, the Officers intending when an opportunity occurred to open communication with the Grand Lodge, if that body was still in existence, and pay such dues as that body might require.

Shortly after the June communication it became known through the profane that a visitor from the Grand Lodge would soon appear and demand the Warrant.

Shortly afterward the Senior Grand Warden arrived in accordance with the following extract from the minutes of the Grand Lodge:

"Grand Lodge of the State of New York,
Annual Meeting, June, A. L. 5847.

Resolved, That R. W. Bro. E. S. Barnum, Senior Grand Warden, be authorized and requested to demand and receive the Warrant and property of the late Otsego Lodge, No. 41, at Cooperstown.

Extract from the minutes.   R. R. Boys, Gd. Sec'y.

He appeared at a regular meeting, and in the name of the Grand Lodge demanded the surrender of the Warrant.

After due consideration it was decided, for the time being, to refuse, fearing that a compliance would forfeit the real estate to the State, and a compromise was finally made to stay the proceedings by referring the matter to the M. W. Grand Master.

Correspondence followed, when it was ascertained that this Lodge, with many others, was stricken from the Grand Lodge list in 1839, for the non-payment of dues, a fact which was entirely unknown to the members of this Lodge.

Meetings were at once discontinued, except such as were necessary for reorganizing, and a delegate was sent to confer with the Grand Lodge, who failed in making a compromise.

December 21st, 1847, a committee, consisting of Bro's Seth Doubleday and James Hyde, was appointed to confer with the M. W. Grand Master, who prayed that under the peculiar circumstances of the case,—the brethren having acted in good faith, and if errors had been committed they were unintentional—the present Warrant might be revived and continued, if, in the opinion of the Grand Lodge, it could constitutionally be done, and if not, that a new Warrant be granted as a renewal or continuance of the old one, that the real estate owned by the Lodge might be continued to it, and preserved and devoted to the Masonic purposes for which it was intended.

Their prayers were heard, as the following endorsement on the old Warrant shows:

"In Grand Lodge of the State of New York, June 8th, 1848, it was Resolved, That a new Warrant be granted to Otsego Lodge No. 41 in continuance of the old Warrant, on payment of the constitutional fee.

That Ariel Thayer be named thereon as Master, James L. Fox as Senior Warden, and Eliab P. Byram, Junior Warden. And under the peculiar circumstances of the case, said Lodge is also allowed to retain its old Warrant, with an endorsement written on its face that a new Warrant has been issued in continuation thereof.

Transactions of Grand Lodge, page 55."

Across the face of the old Warrant is written:

"This Warrant having been surrendered to the Grand Lodge, a new one under the number 138 has been issued in its stead.

Otsego Lodge will hereafter work under the new Warrant, as this is no longer in force.   R. R. Boys, Grand Sec'y."

The new Warrant, under date of June 17th, 1848, bears the seal of the Grand Lodge and the signatures of J. D. Willard, Grand Master; Oscar Coles, Deputy Grand Master; Ezra S. Barnum, Junior Grand Warden, and R. R. Boys, Grand Sec'y.

With the above named Warrant and forty-four members labor was resumed.

An election of officers was held Dec. 21, 1847, yet nothing could be done until fellowship had been restored by the Grand Lodge at its annual communication in June, 1848.

The Hall and property having suffered through neglect, an informal meeting was held June 20, 1848, at which a Committee was appointed to direct and superintend such needful repairs in and about the premises as the state of the treasury would admit, one hundred dollars being expended. The by-laws were revised and prepared for adoption when it might legally be done.

August 8th, 1848, Wor. Bro. James Hyde, having been appointed by R. W. Ezra S. Barnum, Junior Grand Warden, in his stead to install the officers of this Lodge under the name and style of Otsego Lodge No. 138, the new Warrant and Constitution having been read, installed the officers as elected December 21, 1847.

June 2, 1849, the proposed amendments to the Constitution of the Grand Lodge were submitted to this Lodge, and being approved, their adoption was recommended.

Nov. 18th, 1849, Otsego Lodge, No. 106, I. O. of O. F., desired to use the Hall for their meetings, but their committee and that of this Lodge could not make changes in the building to give equal satisfaction to both Orders, so the project was abandoned.

January 22d, 1850, the Lodge donated five dollars to Canajoharie Lodge, which had suffered loss by fire, and a like amount to Warren Lodge No. 147, under like circumstances, February 26, 1850.

April 28, 1850, the Odd Fellows joined with the Lodge in a meeting in the Hall, and attended the funeral of Bro. Richard Cooley and conducted a union service at the grave.

July 23d, 1850, the Lodge accepted an invitation from the Odd Fellows to join with them in holding funeral obsequies in respect to the memory of President Zachary Taylor, and appointed a committee to make the necessary arrangements.

A Brother having appeared at times in the Lodge the worse for his habits of intemperance, was sent a letter of admonition and charges were preferred against another for knowingly having passed counterfeit money on a brother, for which, after due investigation, he was formally expelled from the Lodge.

May 13th, 1851, resolutions were passed directing the representative in Grand Lodge, (if, in his judgment, after being better informed), to favor the project of erecting an Asylum, etc., the committee of the Lodge having approved of its erection, provided the details were satisfactory.

The observance of St. John's day, June 24, 1852, is thus recorded:

"Pursuant to a motion a very large number of Brethren assembled at the Hall. A procession was formed and proceeded to the Presbyterian church, where Bro. J. D. Hammond delivered an address.

After services in the church, procession returned to the Hall, where a vote of thanks was tendered Bro. Hammond for his address and a copy requested for publication. (A copy thereof has been preserved in the Lodge).

The brethren then proceeded to the Eagle Hotel, kept by Bro. Wm. Lewis, for dinner, etc. The day was propitious and everything passed in a manner giving satisfaction."

June 29, 1852, the record shows:

"By telegraph we learn that our distinguished brother, Hon. Henry Clay, Senator of the United States from the State of Kentucky, died this day at the city of Washington, at 11 o'clock A. M., aged 75 years."

July 27, 1852, the Lodge adopted, "as expressive of its regard for the illustrious dead, etc., a series of resolutions adopted in Grand Lodge, and the Lodge clothed in mourning for ninety days."

While making repairs to the Hall in 1852, it was found necessary to relay the foundation. On removing the corner stone the plate of copper 10x5½ inches was discovered. The stone was relaid the same day and an account entered in the records of the Lodge.

Referring to the resurrection of the Lodge after the Morgan troubles, I quote from a personal letter from the venerable Wor. Brother E. P. Byram, written in September, 1892, on completing his 80th year:

"It may and it may not be known to you that it was thro' my instrumentality the Lodge was relieved from the Morgan incubus and resuscitated into new life and put on the way to its present prosperity, for which I sacrificed both time and money.

The old Lodge room never was carpeted, and the only seats were coarse benches, one row against the wall on both sides, and about two feet from them were other benches on both sides of the room, with a shelf on the back side near the top, from which we took our refreshments, which in early days were never omitted, and all we had to do was to turn in our seats and face the lunch, and help ourselves. I broached the subject of resurrecting the Lodge to several of my friends with whom I had pleasant associations, among them Dr. F. G. Thrall, Dr. Wm. H. McNamee, Wm. K. Bingham, Edwin Pier, two brothers Thayer, who were merchants from Poughkeepsie, one of them a Mason, and some I cannot recall. I then proposed to the old members of the Lodge to give us initiation, to which they gladly consented, and we were soon made Masons, and added a carpet and new furniture throughout.

Before I joined the Lodge they only met once a year, for the old Masons to re-elect themselves officers, so as not to forfeit the charter."

The Lodge failed to hold its annual election of officers in December, 1854, and the election was held by virtue of a dispensation from the Grand Lodge, Jan. 2d, 1855.

July 24th, 1855, the Lodge recommended the petition of Isaac Mann and others for a new Lodge at Richmondville, N.Y.

In 1857 three large charts, viz.: E. A., F. C. and M. M., representing the emblems of those degrees, were painted for the Lodge by Bro. Hillman at a cost of seventy-five dollars. These charts, neatly framed, are still retained by the Lodge.

October 15th, 1861, a committee was appointed to arrange for lighting the hall with gas, which was first used on the 12th of November following.

Par. 7: These three paintings are still hung in the lodge room but are in serious need of restoration. They are unique, and even more rare because they are still intact as a set.

In 1865, for the better accommodation of the fraternity, rooms were rented in the "Phinney Block" on Pioneer street, at one hundred dollars per annum, and the old Hall was abandoned for Lodge purposes.

For many years the annual dues were 50 cents; Jan. 29th, 1867, increased to $1; Dec. 16th, 1863, $1.50, and May 2d, 1882, $2.

January 24th, 1865, a resolution was passed, "that in view of the services rendered the Lodge" by P. M. Charles W. Tomlinson, who was about to remove from the place, "that this Lodge make him a donation of one hundred dollars."

July 4th, 1865, the Lodge was invited to join in procession at a celebration to be held in Cooperstown.

Invitation accepted, and sister Lodges were invited to join with this Lodge, securing a large representation of the fraternity.

August 1st, 1865, consent was given to establish a new Lodge at Schenevus, and September 19th, a committee was appointed to examine the proposed officers, and issue a certificate of recommendation to the Grand Lodge.

August 6th, 1870, and Sept. 19th, 1871, the Lodge was visited by the M. W. Grand Master John H. Anthon.

Feb. 21st, 1871, the Lodge concurred with Otsego Chapter, No. 26, R. A. M., to permit Otsego Council, R. & S. M., to hold their meetings in the Hall, free of rent, they paying their just proportion of bill for fuel and gas, until they were financially able to pay rent.

October 17th, 1871, fifty dollars was contributed from the treasury for the relief of brethren who were sufferers by the Chicago fire, and a committee was appointed, who raised about two hundred dollars for that purpose.

In January, 1872, Bro. Kent Jarvis, 33°, presented his photograph to the Lodge, which was acknowledged by appropriate resolutions.

May 21st, 1872, the W. M. was empowered to purchase new jewels.

In 1872 the salary of the Secretary was fixed at twenty-five dollars, and Organist at fifteen dollars, per annum.

October 27th, 1873, Lodge accepted an invitation from Otsego Lodge No. 103, I. O. of O. F., to attend the funeral of Bro. Edward Edwards, who was murdered in his home by burglars, and it was resolved "to attend in citizen's dress, wearing sprig of evergreen and crape." A large number of brethren from sister Lodges joined with this Lodge.

September 15th, 1874, the brethren presented Wor. Bro. F. A. Goffe, on his return from England, a Past Master's Jewel.

Bro. L. H. Hills made the presentation in appropriate words, to which Bro. Goffe responded with much feeling.

January 19th, 1875, ten dollars was contributed toward defraying the expenses of the dedication of the Temple in New York.

March 2d, 1875, Wor. Bro. F. A. Goffe delivered an address on the "Origin of Freemasonry," a copy of which was requested for publication in the county papers.

January 4th, 1876, thirty dollars was donated from the treasury to complete the fund raised by subscription for a monument for the late Daniel Peck.

The monument, costing one hundred and thirty-five dollars, was erected over his remains in Lakewood Cemetery, in memory of him who had long been a faithful brother, serving the Lodge as Tyler for many years.

May 1st, 1877, a committee was appointed to select and purchase a large double lot in Lakewood Cemetery for Masonic burials.

May 21st, 1878, the Lodge Room was rented for sixty dollars per year.

March 16th, 1880, the following invitation was received and accepted:

"To the Master, Wardens and Brethren of Otsego Lodge, No. 138, F. & A. M., and Otsego Chapter No. 26, R. A. M.:

The undersigned, having been authorized to superintend and direct the building of the new County Court House, are desirous that the corner stone thereof shall be laid with formal and solemn ceremonies, and for that purpose do invite you, with such other organizations as you shall invite to act with you, to lay said corner stone with the ceremonies and established rites of your ancient Order.

Dated Cooperstown, March 15, 1880.
    (Signed)   LUTHER I. BURDITT,
                        H. L. WOOD,
                        LEWIS McCREDY,
                                  Building Committee."

Numerous special meetings were called to perfect the arrangements, and much work devolved on the various committees in making a success of the great demonstration which occurred on the 15th of June, 1880, calling out a large assemblage of people.

The procession moved in the following order:

Bro. Rees G. Williams, acted as Grand Marshall, and Wor. Bro. Walter H. Bunn, Deputy Grand Marshall.
Austin's 10th Regiment Band.
Two Tyler's with drawn swords.
S. J. Temple, Tyler Otsego Lodge No. 138, with drawn sword.
W. C. Keyes and Andrew Shaw, Stewards of Otsego Lodge.
No. 138, with white rods.
Tienuderrah Lodge, No. 605.
Schenevus Valley Lodge, No. 592.
Farmers Lodge, No. 553.
Laurens Lodge, No. 548.
Ford's Bush Band.
Butternuts Lodge, No. 515.
Richfield Springs Lodge, No. 482.
Oneonta Lodge, No. 466.
Evergreen Lodge, No. 363.
Schenevus Valley Band.
Cherry Valley Lodge, No. 334.
Freedom Lodge, No. 324.
Otego Union Lodge, No. 282.
Schuyler's Lake Lodge, No. 162.
Utica City Band.
Utica Commandery, No. 3, K. T.
Otsego Lodge, No. 138.

Grand Tyler with drawn sword, Wor. Bro. John E. Hethrington.
Grand Stewards with white rods,
Wor. Bro. James E. Cook, Wor. Bro. Wm. H. Morris.
Brother bearing Golden Vessel containing Corn,
Bro. Bartlett Rogers.
H. G. Wood, Principal Architect, with Square,
Level and Plumb.
Brothers bearing vessels containing Wine and Oil,
Bro. Wm. Temple, Bro. Rufus Wikoff.
R. W. Bro. S. R. Stewart, Grand Secretary.
R. W. Bro. F. G. Bolles, Grand Treasurer.
The Holy Bible, Square and Compasses, borne by a Master of a
Lodge, Wor. Bro. O. F. Lane, supported by two Stewards,
Bro. W. H. Lynes, Bro. John W. Smith.
Two large Lights borne by two Masters, Wor. Bro. J. S.
Loveland, Wor. Bro. H. Hurlburt.
Rt. Wor. and Most Rev. W. W. Lord, Grand Chaplain.
County Judge, Surrogate, District Attorney, County Clerk and
other Judicial Officers.
Board of Supervisors.
Building Committee.
Trustees of the Village.
Rt. Wor. Bro. F. A. Goffe, Junior Grand Warden.
Rt. Wor. Bro. C. B. Foster, Senior Grand Warden.
M. W. Edmond L. Judson, Deputy Grand Master.
Rt. Wor. Bro. James Bowes, with Book of Constitutions.
Grand Deacons, with black rods,
Wor. Bro. C. Ackerman, Wor. Bro. L. S. Henry.
M. W. Jesse B. Anthony, Grand Master.
Two Stewards with white rods.

As the procession arrived at the ground, a sudden and hard shower swept over the village, delaying and somewhat abbreviating the ceremonies.

An Installation Ode was sung by Mrs. Fish, Mrs. Stevenson, Mrs. Eldred, Mrs. Wight, Miss Holmes, Prof. Mildner, E. P. Cory, James Russell, Albert Pierce, Charles B. Gorham, Bro's J. G. Wight, L. H. Hills and E. A. Potter, after which the

Corner Stone,—a block of Berlin Ohio buff sandstone, two feet square by three feet six inches long, weighing over twenty-two hundred pounds, the face of which was embelished with the Egyptian figures "1880"—was laid by M. W. Jesse B. Anthony, with the ancient ceremonies of the Order.

A Dedication Ode was sung, followed by the Grand Master's address to the assemblage, and the Benediction of the Grand Chaplain.

Owing to the inclement weather, the able address prepared by Judge Hezekiah Sturges was omitted, being afterwards published in the county papers.

A copper box, twenty by ten by four inches, filled with interesting articles, principally historical, was placed in the stone and covered with a marble slab inscribed, "June 15th, 1880. M. W. Jesse B. Anthony, Grand Master of the State of New York."

September 14th, 1881, resolutions were passed on the death of Bro. James A. Garfield, President of the United States.

From March 21st, 1882, to August, 1882, by consent of the M. W. Grand Master, the communications were held at Odd Fellows' Hall on Main street while the building in which the Lodge Room is situated was undergoing repairs.

January 4th, 1884, Bro's Gardner, Burnett, Pank, Hyde, McGown and Wikoff accompanied the remains of our late Senior Warden, Alfred Gorringe, to Utica, where Utica Commandery, No. 3, K. T., took charge of the remains and conducted the burial services.

In appreciation thereof, Mrs. Gorringe afterwards presented to the Lodge a picture of Bro. Gorringe.

December 16th, 1884, the members presented Wor. Bro. Addison Gardner a Master's Apron of lamb-skin, appropriately embossed, Bro. Sam'l S. Edick making the presentation in appropriate words.

March 17th, 1885, a committee was appointed to act in conference with a committee from Otsego Chapter to refurnish the Lodge Room.

The work was completed in September, at a cost of nearly

eight hundred dollars, shared equally between the Lodge and Chapter.

The rooms were described in the village papers, abbreviated as follows:

"The floor of the vestibule was covered with new linoleum, and the room contained a new stove and other fixtures.

Upon the floors of the Lodge Room and its annex is an elegant pattern of five-frame body brussels carpet, with border.

The ceilings and walls showed good taste in decorative art.

Elegant new curtains, handsomely rodded, hang at the many windows in the room. Drapery, harmonizing with the curtains at the windows, formed a rich relief background for the chairs of the Officers, five in number, which are ancient specimens of furniture, and had not been re-covered since 1803, as a card found in the lining of one of them indicated, but now looking as good as new, having been thoroughly renovated.

A number of new, large easy cane chairs have been placed in the room, and upon the wall hung a handsome clock.

On the Altar lay a copy of the Bible, nearly a century old, having been printed in 1791.

In the annex is a commodious wardrobe, in which the paraphernalia of the Order is kept.

The woodwork is finished in imitation of cherry.

A new tin roof has been placed over the Hall, and the rooms are well ventilated, and lighted with gas.

Groups of pictures hang on the walls, portraying the faces of different members of the Lodge, among which are Kent Jarvis, S. A. Bowen, W. C. Keyes, Seth Doubleday, W. G. S. Hall, Abner Graves, Ariel Thayer, Harry Metcalf, Daniel Temple, William Lewis, Alfred Gorringe, and many others who have passed to the Lodge beyond."

In a prominent position hangs an elegantly engrossed testimonial from Eastern Star Lodge, No. 227, of New York City, bearing date of Oct. 3d, 1877, thanking the brethren of Otsego Lodge for their care and attention to their Bro. James McNelly, who sickened and died in Cooperstown, and was buried by the Lodge in their lot in Lakewood Cemetery.

Par. 13: The testimonial from Eastern Star Lodge No. 227 is a beautiful example of calligraphy and the lost art of text as functional decoration. It still hangs in the lodge room today.

A quaint old painting, of large size, in the form of a Masonic chart, hangs in the vestibule.

It is very ancient, but nothing in the records show its origin, and the oldest members have no knowledge of its history.

June 24th, 1884, the Lodge attended the laying of the corner stone of the new Masonic Hall at Schenevus, N. Y., in response to an invitation from Schenevus Lodge, No, 592.

About eight hundred Masons were in line, and the interesting ceremonies of the Order were conducted by Deputy Grand Master Frank R. Lawrence. Otsego Lodge was represented by about forty members, and was the oldest Lodge but one present.

June 18th, 1885, by invitation of Oneonta Lodge, No. 466, the Lodge attended the laying of the Corner Stone of the new State Armory at Oneonta.

The attendance of Masonic and other bodies was large, and the ceremonies were ably conducted by Deputy Grand Master John W. Vrooman.

Feb. 25, 1886, a Masonic Ball was held at the Central Hotel in Cooperstown, being referred to by a correspondent of a city newspaper as "one of the most elaborate entertainments ever given here. Crumwell's full band furnished music. Each member wore white gloves and Masonic apron. At 9.30 P. M. the music started with a promenade, and from then till 11:30 dancing was in order.

At midnight an elegant banquet was served."

Pursuant to a resolution, the "Phinney Block" on Pioneer street, occupied by the Lodge, was purchased by H. L. Hinman, William Brooks and John Pank, "as Trustees of Otsego Lodge, No. 138, to be held by them and their successors in office," for $5,500.

This purchase was ratified at a regular communication of the Lodge, March 6th, 1886.

The old Hall on Lake street was sold, netting $2,000, which was applied on payment for the new block.

A resolution was adopted requiring the Lodge and Chapter to pay fifty dollars each to the Trustees for yearly rent, which was continued until Dec. 18th, 1888, when the Hall was offered to those bodies by the Trustees,—approved by a vote of the Lodge,—free of rent.

Par. 1: The "quaint old painting" still hangs in the lodge Club Room. Like the set of three previously noted, it is in serious need of restoration. It is a typical style for the late 18th century, but its age and size make it a true Masonic treasure. (An image appears on page 4.)

December 21st, 1886, a beautiful "Trowel Inkstand" was presented to the Lodge by Bro. Charles R. Burch.

Feb. 21st, 1888, the Hall was lighted with electric light.

March 6th, 1888, the Lodge was officially visited by Rt. Wor. Horace E. Allen, D. D. G. M., at which meeting active measures were taken for the payment of its proportion of the Hall and Asylum debt, amounting to eight hundred forty dollars, which was consummated in the full payment of the same to the Grand Lodge, in May, 1888.

In conformity to an Encyclical issued by M. W. Frank R. Lawrence, Grand Master, that all Lodges in the State meet on the 24th day of April, 1889, at 8 o'clock P. M., to celebrate the payment in full of the Hall and Asylum fund debt, the brethren assembled at Masonic Hall and held commemorative exercises as follows:

1. PRAYER— By Rev. Bro. ROBERT GRANGER, as Chaplain
2. SINGING— *"Old Hundred,"* - - Lodge
    Be Thou, O God, exalted high,
    And as Thy Glory fills the sky,
    So shalt Thou be on earth display'd,
    Till Thou art here as there obeyed.
3. TABLEAU— - "Unveiling the Mysteries, or The Assassination of the Master Builder"
4. READING the Grand Master's Address, Bro. J. G. WIGHT
5. MUSIC— - "Inspire," - - Orchestra
6. TABLEAU— - - "War with the Ephraimites"
7. ADDRESS— - - - Bro. A. C. TENNANT
8. SINGING— "The New Kingdom," Bro. E. A. POTTER
9. TABLEAU— - - "Canceling the Debt, or the Last Bonds Delivered"
10. ADDRESS— - - Wor. Bro. W. H. BUNN
11. MUSIC— - "Forget Me Not," - Orchestra
12. PRESENTATION of Commemorative Medal sent to this Lodge by R. W. Alfred B. Price, and reading of accompanying letter,
    Wor. Bro. A. GARDNER
13. MUSIC— - "Little Dove," - Orchestra
14. TABLEAU— - - - "Locating the Asylum"
15. OVERTURE— - - - - Orchestra
16. BENEDICTION— - - - - Chaplain

Par. 1: This trowel inkstand is a fine example of fraternal material culture and is on display in the lodge Club Room.

A telegram was forwarded to the Grand Master, extending the fraternal congratulations of this Lodge on the success of his long continued efforts to liquidate the debt.

Brethren formed in procession and proceeded to the New Central Hotel, Bro. Olcott McCredy, Proprietor, where the following programme was observed:

1. SINGING— - "Auld Lang Syne," - Brethren
2. OVERTURE— - - - - - - Orchestra
3. INVOCATION— - - - - - - Chaplain

About seventy Brethren were then seated at a grand banquet, and two hours were passed in feasting and social intercourse.

The Annual Convention for the exemplification of work and lectures, for the 18th District, was held with this Lodge, September 2d and 3d, 1890.

R. W. George H. Raymond, Grand Lecturer, who had served in that capacity for a quarter of a century, conducted the Convention, assisted by R. W. Horace E. Allen, D. D. G. M. The session was a pleasant and profitable one, and was largely attended, over twenty Lodges being represented.

M. W. John W. Vrooman, Grand Master, was present on the evening of the 3d, and delivered an able address in Firemen's Hall, the Lodge Room being inadequate to accommodate the brethren.

The Convention closed with a banquet at the Central Hotel, at which over one hundred brethren did ample justice to the excellent menu prepared for them at the expense of the brethren of Otsego Lodge.

December 2d, 1890, book-marks for the Bible were purchased of Cattaraugus Lodge, No. 239, to aid said Lodge, which had suffered loss by fire.

Dec. 16, 1890, Bro. Henry H. Hill, of Mistletoe Lodge, No. 647, Brooklyn, N. Y., (afterward an affiliate with Otsego Lodge), presented the Lodge a beautiful nickel gong, inscribed:

"Presented by Henry H. Hill of Mistletoe Lodge No. 647, F. & A. M., to Otsego Lodge, No. 138, F. & A. M."

February 17, 1891, R. W. Horace E. Allen, D. D. G. M.,

Par. 9: The nickel gong (actually more like a bell from a boxing ring) is still used in lodge degree rituals.

officially visited the Lodge and presented the initiate of the evening,—Bro. Alvin Van Dewalker,—with an apron of lambskin, suitably inscribed, it being the first gift of an apron to a candidate in this Lodge. The custom was continued.

May 21st, 1891, a number of brethren attended the laying of the corner stone of the Masonic Home at Utica, which was the largest assemblage of Masons ever seen in New York State.

Otsego Lodge united with adjoining Lodges and secured the services of the "Homer City Band," its proportion of the expense being forty dollars.

November 4th, 1891, R. W. Horace E. Allen, D. D. G. M., committed suicide by drowning near his home in Binghamton, on the notice of which the Hall was draped in mourning. Arrangements were made for special trains, and a number of brethren attended the funeral services in Binghamton, Sunday P. M., Nov. 7th, it being one of the largest and most impressive Masonic funerals ever held in the State.

The day was warm and fair, and fully ten thousand people assembled in the cemetery to listen to the impressive burial service of the order.

Bro. Erastus F. Beadle received the first degree in Masonry June 22, 1847, the second degree August 22, 1890, and on the 1st day of December, 1891, the third degree, a case without a parallel in the records of Masonry in the State.

At the annual communication of the Lodge, held December 18th, 1894, the following was offered and unanimously adopted:

"Whereas, The One Hundredth Anniversary of the granting of the charter to Otsego Lodge by the Grand Lodge of the State of New York, will occur on the 14th day of August, 1895, it is fitting that the event should be celebrated with appropriate ceremonies; therefore

Resolved, That a committee consisting of Bro's Addison Gardner, D. Jefferson McGown, John Pank, Otis H. Babbitt and Albert T. Van Horne be appointed, with power to make the necessary arrangements for such celebration, and to appoint such sub-committees as they shall deem necessary, the appointment of such committees to be subject to the approval of the Lodge."

In conformity to the above, the Centennial Celebration of the day of the granting of the Charter was celebrated on the 14th of August with appropriate ceremonies. An invitation was extended to the several Lodges in the county, the Masters of all other Lodges in the 18th District, Officers of the Grand Lodge, and many other Masons of prominence.

Among those present were M. W. John Stewart, Grand Master; R. W. James S. Manning, Grand Marshall; R. W. John R. Pope, Grand Lecturer; R. W. Emera A. Cobb, D. D. G. M. of the 18th District; R. W., S. D. Affleck, D. D. G. M. of the 7th District; R. W. Oscar F. Lane, Past D. D. G. M of the 18th District, and Most Rev. Wm. W. Lord, D. D., Past Grand Master of the Grand Lodge of Mississippi.

The brethren assembled at Masonic Hall at 7 P. M. and proceeded in procession to Firemen's Hall, where the public exercises were held.

After the reception of the Grand Officers, the following programme was carried out, Wor. Bro. Walter H. Bunn presiding:

ORDER OF EXERCISES.

MARCH— - - - - - Orchestra

AIR—*Boylston*.
Oh! God, we come to thee;
Hear Thou our fervent prayer;
May all our work accepted be
And we Thy blessing share. —*Nohrvan*.

PRAYER— - - M. Rev. W. W. LORD, Chaplain
READING of the Original Charter, - -
- - Wor. Bro. ANDREW DAVIDSON
MUSIC— - - Flute Solo, - Mr. L. N. WOOD
READING the History of Otsego Lodge, No. 138. (Written by Wor. Bro. Albert T. Van Horne).
Wor. Bro. WALTER H. BUNN

ANTHEM—	- "Send out Thy Light,"	-	*Gounod*
ADDRESS—	- -	Wor. Bro. WALTER H. BUNN	
ADDRESS—	- -	M. W. Bro. JOHN STEWART	
ANTHEM—	- "Magnificat,"	-	- *Simper*
POEM—	- "Time's Touch,"	- Bro. CHARLES W. ALLEN	

AIR—*Old Hundred.*

    Be Thou, O God, exalted high,
    And as Thy glory fills the sky,
    So shalt Thou be on earth displayed,
    Till Thou art here as there obeyed.

BENEDICTION— - M. Rev. W. W. LORD, Chaplain

The short prelude to the prayer, composed by the Secretary of the Lodge, for the occasion, was sung by the audience, followed by an eloquent invocation by the Chaplain of the evening, Most Rev. W. W. Lord.

An interesting feature was the reading of the Original Charter, bearing date of August 14th, 1795, by Wor. Andrew Davidson.

Wor. Walter H. Bunn read the History of the Lodge, written for the occasion by Wor. Albert T. Van Horne, which briefly reviewed the more important events from the date of organization to the present time, showing its eras of prosperity and adversity, which was listened to with manifest interest by the fraternity. From information obtained from the elder members, who have long since been raised to that Lodge which shall never close, a vivid description of the Lodge Room of other days was portrayed, and customs of early times were described. Of the thirty-five who have held the office of Master, but thirteen were living, ten of whom were present.

The address by Wor. Walter H. Bunn was eloquent, able and instructive, embracing interesting historical facts, civil, political and Masonic, showing careful study and research on the part of the speaker, and was listened to with deep attention.

Bro. Chas. W. Allen read an original poem, entitled "Time's Touch," which was a brilliant composition and merited the applause of the large audience.

The flute solo by Mr. L. N. Wood, and vocal and instrumental selections by the chorus and orchestra, under the direction of Bro. Covell S. Derrick, were pleasing features of the evening.

M. W. John Stewart delivered a brief address on the subject of "Freemasonry," saying in conclusion: "It is with more than usual interest that I come from a distant part of the State, to speak a word of encouragement to you and bid you God speed in the commencement of another century of Masonic work. May it be even more profitable than the first. May prosperity be yours, remaining true to the Great Fraternity whose foundation is Truth; whose tenets are 'Friendship, Morality and Brotherly Love,' and whose cap-stone is inscribed 'Holiness to the Lord.'"

It was a source of regret, quite generally expressed, that he did not make a more extended address.

The Hall was tastefully decorated with evergreens and century plants, under the direction of Bro. James G. Parshall.

At the conclusion of the exercises the brethren repaired to the apparatus room below, where an elaborate banquet was served by the wives and daughters of the Masons, assisted by other members of their families, the refreshments being contributed by the members of the Lodge.

The following Toasts were named by Bro. B. P. Ripley, Toast-master, and responded to in a pleasant manner by the brethren:

"The Grand Lodge of the State of New York," R. W. Jas. S. Manning.

"Otsego Lodge, No. 138," Wor. Walter H. Bunn.

"Our Visiting Brethren," R. W. Oscar F. Lane.

"The Masonic Fraternity," Wor. Myron A. McKee.

"The Ladies," Wor. Andrew Davidson.

"Our Past Masters," Wor. Lyman H. Hills.

On the tables were the two famous columns, beautifully wrought in flowers, and a profusion of cut flowers contributed by the ladies.

The following morning the visiting brethren who had remained over night, together with the resident members and their families, were invited by the committee to join in an excursion around Otsego Lake on the steamer "Natty Bumppo," stopping on the return at Three Mile Point, where a lunch was served by the ladies of the party.

About seventy were present, and several hours were pleasantly passed.

Carriages conveyed the Grand Officers to the three o'clock train, and the remainder of the party returned by steamer, thus closing the celebration, which visitors and members alike voted an unqualified success.

Cornerstone from the original Otsego Lodge building, 1797.
The chiseled inscription reads, "A.L. 5797".

Copper plate inscribed by Elihu Phinney and set into the original cornerstone.
A discussion of the Latin text and its translation can be found on page 68.

Van Horne's Updated History (1906)

During the ten years following his centennial history, Albert T. Van Horne served as Secretary from 1900-1904 and was the first member ever listed in the lodge records as Historian (1906-1913). He must have enjoyed success with his centennial history, or at least received due recognition for the usefulness of that book, because ten years later he followed it up with an updated history. It may have been his intent that subsequent lodge historians would continue that tradition, but alas, it was not.

The 1906 addendum was physically no more than a pamphlet. It measures 6 x 8 inches in size, with a gray-blue paper cover set in navy type. The 24 pages are stapled and printed on a heavy stock, glossier than that of the centennial edition. The volume bears the imprint of "1906 CRIST, SCOTT & PARSHALL, Cooperstown N. Y." on the back cover. The reverse of the title page displays a potrait of Van Horne (reproduced here on page 6), with "Fraternally Yours," and a facsimile of his signature underneath. He appears prosperous and dapper, in that late 19th-century sort of way, complete with handlebar moustache. The dedication on the third page reads:

To the brethren with whom we have labored in Masonry for a quarter of a century, this volume is fraternally dedicated.

It remains a curiosity that the dedications of both of Van Horne's volumes leave the word "fraternally" hyphenated.

There is also a photograph on the fourth page with the caption, "Masonic Hall, Erected 1797." The image depicts the first Otsego Lodge hall, still located on the northeast corner of Lake and Pioneer streets. A man stands in the left foreground, too small to reliably identify, but presumably it is either Van Horne or the contemporary owner of the building, which was a private residence at that time.

The cover and title page show that the pamphlet contained more than what is reproduced here in this current volume. As stated before, the additional information will be considered in the forthcoming full history in 2011. The following is a list of the full contents of the 1906 history, including the actual chapter titles and relevant short commentary (in parentheses).

- History of Otsego Lodge, No. 138, F. & A. M., Cooperstown, N. Y. (Reproduced here in full, without the original page numbers to avoid confusion with page numbers in this current volume.)
- Officers of Otsego Lodge. (These tables include the entire set of each year's officers, 1896-1906, as does the other list below.)
- Members of Otsego Lodge (Listed by year of lodge initiation or affiliation.)
- History of Otsego Chapter, No. 26, R. A. M., Cooperstown, N. Y.
- Officers of Otsego Chapter No. 26 and Date of Their Election.

- Members of Otsego Chapter No. 26.
- Order Eastern Star. (The O. E. S. is a concordant body within the greater Masonic family. It admits both Masons and women, and is still active in Cooperstown today. This is not really a book chapter, but a two-paragraph synopsis of its brief history from 1900.)
- Knights of Birmingham. (Also just two paragraphs, Van Horne describes it as a "side degree" for Master Masons, organized in Cooperstown in 1883. Now defunct, the group numbered nearly 200 in 1906.)
- In Memoriam. (A one-page chapter, prefaced by three stanzas of poetry, and containing what appears to be an inclusive list of deceased members from the previous decade.)

Some of Van Horne's commentary is slightly redundant, which he tried to avoid (and apologized for). Within that redundancy, some of the "new" information, when read together with the 1896 history, is somewhat confusing. An example is his statement about the lodge moving from Phinney's house to that of Samuel Huntington and mentioning the erection of the Eagle Hotel. It is a little misleading because at the time, the Red Lion Tavern was located there and the Eagle Hotel was not erected until decades later. (Although it may be that Huntington, as proprietor, also lived in the tavern.) At any rate, such discrepancies will have to be reconciled in the full history in 2011.

Much of what Van Horne adds is social in nature, describing more of the celebrations and funerals than hardcore history. That is to be suspected in such a relatively short span of a just a decade in the life of a prosperous organization. The regular mundane operations are often deemed not worth reporting.

He does make some odd comments, such as the one regarding females being the foes of Freemasonry (last paragraph, page 43). Obviously the opposite is true; there is abundant evidence that wives and female family members have been overwhelmingly supportive of the Cooperstown Freemasons over the years and is still true today.

HISTORY

OF

OTSEGO LODGE
NO. 138, F. & A. M.

AND

OTSEGO CHAPTER
No. 26, R. A. M.

COOPERSTOWN, N. Y.

HISTORY OF FREEMASONRY

EMBRACING

Otsego Lodge No. 138, F. & A. M.
Otsego Chapter No. 26, R. A. M.

1896 to 1906

By
ALBERT T. VAN HORNE

Cooperstown, N. Y., March 1st, 1906

History of Otsego Lodge, No. 138, F. & A. M., Cooperstown, N. Y.

MASONIC researches during the past decade have brought to light some treasures in Masonry, some of which "had lain buried in darkness" for a century or more and "without a knowledge of which" the history of Otsego Lodge would be incomplete.

From ancient papers obtained from friends, together with others among the archives, some items are revealed which do not appear on the imperfectly kept records of the Lodge of a century ago.

In presenting them, it may be necessary to partially repeat some articles in the Centennial History, for which we crave the indulgence of the reader.

Inclusive of the eleven members present at the first "regular meeting" held March 1st, 1796, (Bro. P. Parker being a "visitor"), the membership of the Lodge at the close of the year by affilliation and initiation numbered seventy-three, twelve being added in the month of December, the work of ten months, very largely exceeding that of any succeeding year in the history of the Lodge.

Its prosperity continued and at the close of 1797 the membership had increased to one hundred and three and continued to flourish until the cessation of work in 1827, when the total admissions numbered three hundred and eighty-one.

In the month of August, 1796, the Lodge was moved "from the dwelling of Worshipful Bro. E. Phinney on Second St" (now Main) "to the house of Bro. Samuel Huntington, S. W. corner of Second and West Sts." (now Main and Pioneer) on which site the Eagle Hotel was afterward erected, where it remained until the completion of the new Masonic Hall.

Pursuant to a resolution of the Lodge, the Masonic Hall was "raised" on the 24th of June, 1797, and tradition relates that not a loud word was spoken upon the ground nor a metal tool used on this interesting occasion.

The opening of the year 1804 was signalized by the reception of a poetical New Year's Address from unknown hands directed to the "Worshipful Master of Otsego Lodge, Cooper's-Town."

It has many times been said that the ladies are, and ever have been the foes of Free masonry, but this has not been true, of all, at least when speaking of the ladies of Cooperstown as this tribute of their "artless friendship" will plainly evince. The names of the three "*dillentanti*" if ever known to Masons are now forever lost.

By order of the Lodge, a copy thereof was delivered to Bro. Samuel Huntington with a request that he should set the same to *music*, but nothing appears to show that this request was complied with.

"To the Masons of Otsego Lodge No. 40:

Gentlemen:—We have often observed, that when a member of your society ascends the throne of eloquence to address his listening Brethren, the Ladies are generally indebted to the politeness of the Orator for remarks made particularly to them, which speak the sentiments of esteem and friendship.

We know not that custom has ever yet licensed a female to return an acknowledgment for the attention your affability bestows on her—but we wish not to suppress the effusions of gratitude, and trust you will excuse us, when we beg you to accept the sincere wishes of three female friends.

MARIA, LORENDIA, OLIVIA.

A dawning year breaks through the night,
And turns each heart to pure delight;
    Hope dances in each eye—
Each to a friend his wishes bear,
That happiness may crown the year
    With its attendant joy.

Prompted by true sincerity,
With pleasure and timidity,
    We follow custom's way;
And to the friends of all mankind,
We wish felicity refined
    May bless each future day.

If happiness from wisdom flows,
If virtue e'er the boon bestows,
    Or bliss with friendship rest;
If knowledge leads to sparkling joys,
And malice ne'er your peace destroys,
    You are already blest.

As your benevolence extends
To strangers, enemies or friends,
    Who feel misfortune's dart;
And as your goodness pleasures give,
May you in turn the same receive—
    True pleasures of the heart.

When friendship draws her circling zone,
When science claims ideas her own,
    And points to Masonry;
While you pursue the mazy road,
That leads to Wisdom and to God,
    May all your thoughts be free.

But when from busy scenes retir'd
When with domestic peace inspired
    And calm content renew'd,
Think—that a soul will sometimes warm,
And animate a woman's form,
    Which glows with gratitude.

Self-approbation is reward;
Yet virtue claims a due regard,
    Though clothed in mystery;
A humane heart you never hide—
We view alone the charming side,
    Admiring Masonry.

These lines with diffidence we send;
By artless friendship they are penn'd;
    We wish you to forget
The incorrectness of each line;
Remember only the design,
    Where awe and feeling met.

A happy year still echoes round,
Our hearts reverberate the sound;
    May you its sweets enjoy;
May fortune every blessing lend,
And science all its charms extend,
    To give each hour employ."

January 1st, 1804."

To show the rigid adherence of the Lodge to its By-laws, is a resolution that "the Brother, who, acting as Secretary *pro-tem*, received a promissory note in lieu of the initiation fees, be requested to pay the amount thereof into the hands of the Treasurer immediately, the Lodge refusing to accept the note."

The year 1817 was somewhat remarkable for the incidents which agitated the Lodge for some time and proved the efficiency of Masonic law when appealed to for the adjustment of difficulties whether between Brother and Brother or the Lodge and a portion of its members. The several proceedings were quite prolonged and as far as permissible in the records, are now to be found in the archives of the Lodge.

Toward the close of 1826, some few of the members of the Lodge, becoming restless under the proscriptions of political anti-masonry, appeared in a body and notified the Worshipful Master, of their intention, at the approaching regular meeting of the Lodge, to move for a surrender of its Warrant, as a step calculated to appease public opinion, and allay the excitement which was then beginning to rage throughout the State. To this the Worshipful Master replied in substance that he did not consider it to be a favored question—and he would refuse to entertain it before the Lodge, unless all of its members were previously notified of the intention, and so long as he remained the depository of the Warrant and was sustained by the constitutional number of masons, he would never consent to surrender the Warrant for such a purpose.

He further observed, that if they concurred he would call the meeting to be held at an early hour, and then informally consider what might be done under the then existing state of public feeling; and whatever might be determined on by the Brethren so assembled, short of a surrender of the Warrant, he for one would cheerfully observe.

It was afterwards informally agreed, that as an experiment, this Lodge would cease from its labors,—keep its property insured and its standing good in Grand Lodge—and to meet only for the purpose of closing its unfinished business, and of organization, by the annual election of its officers; or otherwise as circumstances might require. About 1835 the intense persecution of masonry having partially subsided, an attempt was made to resume labor, and a resolution to that effect was passed by a small majority, but those in the minority were so earnest in opposition that it appeared that the time had not yet come and the resolution was allowed to pass by inoperative, and not until 1846 were the meetings regularly held.

After the granting of the new charter, the past proceedings of the Lodge were formally healed by the resolution of the Grand Lodge, and it was thought how much perplexity might have been saved to the Committee and to our delegates, if it had only occurred to either of them, that Sec. 3 of Art. CV of the Constitution of 1845 was plainly "*ex post facto*" in its operation, and was no rule for their guidance in the case before them.

This Lodge would then have taken its true numerical rank as No. 13 in the "List of Lodges" in the State.

At this time the Grand Lodge did not deal with its subordinates with the lenience shown by those in foreign countries, notably that of the United Grand Lodge of England, in the Constitution of which was the following: "No Lodge shall be erased until the Master or officers of the Lodge shall have been summoned to show cause in Grand Lodge why such sentence should not be recorded and enforced."

As evidence that a Lodge once existed in Springfield we find that in Sept. 1854, "the Lodge was visited by the venerable Samuel Coleman, Esq., aged 86, late a member of 'Rising Sun Lodge No. 135' (old registry, now extinct) once held in that town, in this county." "I wanted to sit in a Lodge once more," were his emphatic words addressed to the Master.

June 6,1857, one of the "Chinese Performers" attached to a traveling circus expressed a desire to see the Masonic Hall. He was introduced by one of our brethren, and in his way expressed much delight, and offered himself for examination. He claimed to have received the first degrees in China. He was found to answer readily as far as the seventh degree and offered himself for examination in the degrees of the "hauts grades," which was declined, presumably from inability on the part of the brothers to conduct the same. He left his address, written in Chinese, which he interpreted to read: "Dor, Me, Gee, from China."

Feb. 3, 1857, the Lodge attended the funeral of Bro. Sumner Ely at his residence in the town of Middlefield, and June 20, a large number of the brethren attended that of Bro. Abram Van Horne in Pierstown, one of the early settlers of the town, who died on the farm where he located in 1802. The services were very impressively renderd by Wor. Bro. E. P. Byram, at the family vault on the farm where he had so long resided. Bro. Van Horne, though not a member of this Lodge, was one of its most loyal supporters during the many dark years of its adversity.

With this digression, we resume the routine history of the Lodge for a decade, which, aside from an era of more than usual prosperity, has been marked with few events that are of more than passing interest to the fraternity. Its membership has been largely increased, and the Standard work has been raised to a degree of perfection that is surpassed by few Lodges in this Grand jurisdiction.

A public Installation of Officers was held Jan. 4th, 1898, at Firemen's Hall, R. W. Dow Beekman, D. D. G. M. of the 18th Masonic District conducting the ceremonies, which were interspersed with music and singing. At the conclusion of the ceremonies, about one hundred Brethren repaired to the Hotel Fenimore where a banquet was served, and after ample justice had been done the excellent menu prepared for the occasion, an hour was pleasantly spent in social intercourse.

The funeral of Wor. Bro. Henry L. Hinman on the 25th of Nov., 1898, was largely attended by members of this and Sister Lodges, and the impressive Templar burial service, was, owing to the inclement weather, conducted at the residence by a large delegation of Knights Templar from Little Falls Commandery No. 26 of which our deceased Brother was a member.

At an expense of about Fifty Dollars, in the summer of 1899, a portion of the second floor of the Hall was re-modeled and furnished for a dining room, where refreshments could be served to about fifty brethren, comfortably seated at tables. Near the close of 1904 the remaining rooms on the same floor became vacant, and acquiring those the seating capacity was materially increased. Improvements continued until the close of the year 1905, consisting mainly of increasing the seating capacity and placing registers for heating the Lodge Room, providing and furnishing a coat room and pantry on the second floor and by the further enlargement and equipment of the dining hall at a cost of about Four Hundred and Forty Dollars.

Oct. 24 and 25, 1899, the annual District Convention for the exemplification of the Standard work, was held in the Hall, conducted by R. W. Bro. W. H. Whiting, assisted by R. W. Charles Smith, D. D. G. M. of the 18th Masonic District, all Lodges in the District being represented, and a large number of Masons sought the benefit of the instruction given.

A steamer was chartered by the Lodge and the visiting Brethren were tendered an excursion around Otsego Lake, the convention closing with a banquet at the Central Hotel.

In accordance with an Encyclical issued by the Grand Lodge, the Brethren assembled at the Hall on the evening of Dec. 31, 1899, for the purpose of attending divine service in commemoration of Wor. Bro. George Washington.

A procession was formed and proceeded to the Presbyterian church, where an able and instructive discourse was delivered by the Pastor, Wor. Bro. Sidney S. Conger on "Lessons from the life of Washington." The Bible borne in the procession, was used at a similar service in Otsego Lodge, Feb. 22, 1800.

Nov. 24, 1899, the organ which had been in use for many years, was replaced with a modern one, the difference in price, viz., $35.00, being met by voluntary contribution from the Brethren.

On the 4th of Jan., 1900, about fifty members of the Lodge went by special train to Schenevus in response to an invitation from Wor. Herbert Bernard, on the occasion of his retiring from the office of Master of Schenevus Valley Lodge No. 592. Many prominent Masons were in attendance, including Dep'y. Grand Master Charles W. Mead, who at the close of an elaborate banquet delivered an address of more than usual interest to the fraternity.

R. W. Charles Smith, D. D. G. M., officially visited the Lodge, Jan. 16, 1900, and assisted in conferring the third degree. Wor. Rev. Sidney

S. Conger, late of New Jersey, gave an illustration of the Standard work in that state, which was very interesting.

In response to an invitation from R. W. Charles Smith, on the 16th of Jan., 1900, about seventy-five Masons went by special train to visit Oneonta Lodge No. 466, the occasion being a reception to M. W. Wright D. Pownell, Grand Master. Over fifty Lodges were represented and six hundred Masons were present at the banquet. R. W. Bro. Smith was presented with a beautiful jewel of his office, the gift of the Lodges of the 18th Dist., Otsego Lodge contributing ten dollars.

The festival of St. John the Baptist was observed June 24, 1900, by attending (on invitation) divine service at the Presbyterian Church, when about fifty of the Brethren listened to an eloquent discourse by the Pastor, Wor. Sidney S. Conger.

In May, 1900, the following resolution by the Building Committee of the Board of Supervisors of Otsego County, was received and accepted.

"*Resolved*—That the Corner Stone of the new County Clerk and Surrogate's Office (at Cooperstown) be laid with Masonic ceremonies, and that Otsego Lodge No. 138 F. & A. M., be, and is hereby invited to perform these ceremonies."

At the following communication of the Lodge, an executive committee consisting of Wor. Brothers Frank Hale, Albert T. Van Horne, Nathaniel P. Willis and Bros. Willard D. Johnson and Edward S. Brockham was appointed, authorized to appoint the necessary sub-committees, and have full charge of all arrangements in behalf of the Lodge, for the ceremonies to be held July 28, 1900.

Invitations were issued to the Grand Lodge, the Lodges in the 18th District and vicinity and several commanderies, most of which were promptly accepted. No more every-way perfect day could have been had for the delight of those interested, and nothing occurred to mar the pleasure of the occasion.

In the procession, led by the 10th Regiment Band of Albany, were over one thousand Masons, with several bands, and a large delegation from Temple Commandery No. 2, K. T. of Albany.

The impressive ceremonies were conducted in ample form by M. W. Charles W. Mead, Grand Master, assisted by the following associate officers:

R. W. Elbert Crandall	Deputy Grand Master.
R. W. John W. Jenkins	as Senior Grand Warden.
R. W. Charles Smith	as Junior Grand Warden.
R. W. Walter M. Hand	as Grand Treasurer.
R. W. Albert C. Goodwin	as Grand Secretary.
R. W. George W. White	Past Grand Treasurer.
R. W. James A. Beckett	Grand Marshal.
R. W. John Laubenheimer	Grand Chaplain.
M. W. William W. Lord	as Grand Chaplain.
R. W. Fred L. Cogshall	D. D. G. M. 18th Dist.

R. W. Herbert E. Bergden	Grand Steward.
R. W. Isaac Hersch	Grand Steward.
R. W. Charles Melius	Grand Steward.
Wor. Nathaniel P. Willis	as Grand Steward.
R. W. Dow Beekman	as Grand Standard Bearer.
R. W. Emera A. Cobb	as Grand Sword Bearer.
R. W. Edwin Buckmas	as Senior Grand Deacon
Wor. William Rose	as Junior Grand Deacon.
R. W. S. Nelson Sawyer	Chief Com'r of Appeals.
R. W. Oscar F. Lane.	Com'r of Appeals.
R. W. Isaac Fromme	Com'r of Appeals.
R. W. A. A. Clark	Grand Librarian.
Wor. R. A. Gunnison	as Grand Pursuviant.
Wor. Andrew Ferguson	Tiler.

The able address by Hon. George W. Ray of Norwich, was listened to with marked attention.

In behalf of the Lodge, Wor. Bro. Frank Hale presented the Grand Master with a costly souvenir trowel appropriately inscribed. The visiting Brethren were received, and assigned to headquarters, and dinner and lunch were served at Firemen's Hall, and after feeding the multitude twice, boxes were sent to the trains for travelers' lunches, and the residue sent to the Orphan House of the Holy Saviour.

The citizens contributed with their usual liberality toward defraying the expenses, and to them, the ladies of Cooperstown, and the members of Flycreek Chapter No. 201, Order Eastern Star, the executive committee were under many obligations for their very liberal contributions, and for the excellent service so freely performed by them at the hall.

The Grand officers remained in town over Sunday and were entertained by R. W. Charles Smith of Oneonta.

On invitation from the Pastor, the Lodge attended divine service at the Baptist church, Sunday evening, July 29th, and listened to an interesting and appropriate sermon by Rev. Chellis E. Nichols on "The Corner Stone" for which a vote of thanks was returned.

In August, 1900, the Lodge was honored by the appointment of Wor. Bro. Frank Hale to the position of Assistant Lecturer.

In 1901, the boxes in the Post Office on the first floor of the Hall were purchased by the Lodge, and a contract was made with the Post Office Department for a lease of the rooms for a term of five years at $550.00 per annum, the Lodge providing fuel and lights.

June 23, 1901, the Lodge attended divine services at the Baptist church on invitation from the Pastor, Rev. Chellis E. Nichols, who delivered an interesting discourse on the theme, "The greatness of Saint John the Baptist." and on the 29th of June, 1902, on invitation a like service was attended at the Universalist Church, the instructive and able discourse being delivered by the Pastor, Rev. Bro. E. A. Perry. Sunday evening, June 21, 1903, about two hundred Masons, including numerous visitors from Sister Lodges, attended

---

Par. 3: The commemorative silver trowel is on display with other ceremonial trowels in the dining hall of the impressive Masonic Temple in Albany, New York.

services commemorative of Saint John the Baptist, at Christ Church, where a most able and instructive Masonic sermon was delivered by Rt. Wor. and Rt. Rev. Henry C. Potter, Bishop of New York.

During 1892, the attention of the Lodge was directed to certain neglected Masonic graves in a school-house yard midway between Cooperstown and Flycreek, several committees being appointed to investigate, who ascertained one to be that of Oliver Gardner, late a member of this Lodge, and another whose Lodge was unknown. Following the recommendations of the committees, a substantial granite marker was placed at the grave of the last named brother, and the original slab reset at the grave of the former, measures being adopted to prevent further desecration.

On information being received that the grave of our late brother, Wor. Eliab P. Byram in Lakewood cemetery was unmarked, the sum of Fifty Dollars was subscribed by a number of the members, and a suitable memorial in dark Barre granite, inscribed in memory of our esteemed brother and wife, was erected in Oct., 1905, for which the sincere thanks of the family were extended to the contributors to the fund.

Feb. 6, 1906, a committee was appointed to solicit funds to erect a suitable marker at the grave of Bro. James McNelly of Eastern Star Lodge No. 277 on the Lodge lot in Lakewood cemetery, or if practicable to procure a monument for the lot, being another illustration of the fact that Masons are not unmindful of their fraternal dead.

On the 6th of May, 1904, the Lodge attended the funeral of our late Bro. Hon. George Van Horn, and the burial services were impressively rendered at the grave in Lakewood cemetery.

Bro. George Van Horn conveyed by will to Otsego Lodge the sum of Five Hundred Dollars, and directed that the amount be applied "to reduce the indebtedness on the Hall, if any should exist at the time of his decease." This we believe to be the first bequest to the Lodge from any of its members.

In June, 1904, the Lodge was honored by the appointment of Wor. Bro. Nathaniel P. Willis to the position of D. D. G. M. of the 18th Masonic District, and as a mark of approval, on the 21st of June, Bro. Willis was escorted to the Lodge by its Past Masters, where after an address of congratulation and welcome, he was presented with an apron appropriate to his official rank, the gift of the Brethren of the Lodge.

Feb. 23, 1903, Article 10 of Sec. 2 of the By-Laws was amended to read: "Every member, except such as are by usage exempt shall annually pay, on or before the first day of November, Two Dollars dues, *excepting that beginning with Nov. 1, 1903, all Master Masons who have been members of the Lodge continuously for twenty years from the date of their consummating their membership, shall pay annual dues of one-half dollar only, payment to be made as prescribed above.*"

The stated communication held Nov. 1st, 1904, was observed as "Past

Masters' night," the several stations being occupied by Past Masters during the conferring of the third degree.

R. W. Nathaniel P. Willis was introduced and received with the honors due his station. He entered a plea for an amendment to the constitution proposed by the Grand Lodge to levy a per capita tax of Fifty Cents, for the support of the Masonic Home at Utica, N. Y. At a subsequent meeting the recommendation was adopted, the Lodge having been summoned for that purpose.

Oct. 3, 1905, the By-Laws were amended providing that beginning with Nov. 1, 1905, the annual dues should be Two Dollars and Fifty Cents, except that those of continuous membership for twenty years should pay the sum of One Dollar, the increase being made to meet the requirement of the Grand Lodge.

June 4, 1905, services were held in the Presbyterian Church, commemorative of St. John's Day, being held at an earlier date than usual, for the convenience of R. W. Rev. John Laubenheimer, Grand Lecturer of the Grand Lodge of the State of New York, who was present and gave one of the best sermons it had been the privilege of Otsego Lodge to hear, taking for his text, Isaiah 32:2. He was succeeded by R. W. and Rt. Rev. Henry C. Potter, Bishop of New York, who gave interesting reminiscences of his own experience, and pronounced the benediction. An interesting musical program, very impressively rendered, was prepared for the occasion.

Immediately after the conclusion of the services at the church, an informal reception was tendered R. W. Bro. Laubenheimer at the Lodge Room.

Dec. 7, 1905, by invitation, a large delegation of Masons attended a special communication of Oneonta Lodge No. 466, it being the annual "Past Masters' Night." After witnessing the impressive conferring of the 3d degree by the Past Masters, the dining hall was opened, where the banquet board was spread with tempting viands, to which ample justice was done, the brethren returning by special car.

Dec. 19, 1905, was observed by the Lodge as the annual "Past Masters' Night," and a large assemblage of Masons witnessed the conferring of the 3d degree, by those who have wielded the emblem of power in years past, at the close of which the inner man was refreshed at a banquet in the dining hall.

During the past decade the Lodge has responded liberally to the numerous demands for charitable purposes, and the records show that over Seven Hundred Dollars has been given to alleviate suffering, and the respect for the fraternal dead has been manifested by an expenditure of over One Hundred Dollars for floral tributes.

In addition to the above, the sum of $50 was forwarded by the Lodge for the relief of brethren suffering by the destruction of the City of San Francisco by earthquake and fire in April, 1906.

The report of the Lodge Jan. 1, 1906, showed a membership of One

Hundred and Ninety-eight and that the mortgage indebtedness on the Hall was reduced to Five Hundred Dollars. At this time the sum of Two Hundred Dollars was transferred to the Trustees to enable them to meet the indebtedness incurred in making the several improvements in the Hall.

The introduction of the system of free delivery of mail in Cooperstown, Feb. 1, 1906, required a complete re-arrangement on the first floor of the Hall to meet the requirements of the Post Office.

In compliance therewith, the Trustees entered into an agreement with the Post Office Department, whereby the Lodge should replace the present fixtures with those required for the new system of delivery, install a heating plant, refit the present windows with plate glass, provide a safe, lock boxes, etc., refloor and repaint throughout at an estimated cost of about Two Thousand Dollars, and a contract was signed on the 26th of Jan., 1906, leasing the office to the Post Office Department for a term of ten years, at Eight Hundred and Fifty Dollars per annum, the Lodge providing fuel and electric lights.

Feb. 20, 1906, the trustees were authorized by a vote of the Lodge, to install a plant of sufficient capacity to heat the entire building with steam at a cost of $620, thereby increasing the estimated cost of repairs.

A special communication was held March 2, 1906, for the purpose of tendering a farewell reception to Wor. Brother Merton Barnes, who was about to remove to Oklahoma. About one hundred brethren were present, and the evening was pleasantly passed in social intercourse, concluding with a banquet served in the dining hall, where brief remarks were made by a score of the brethren. Wor. Brother Barnes was presented with a beautiful Past Masters' Jewel, valued at forty dollars, the gift of the brethren of the Lodge, R. W. Nathaniel P. Willis making the presentation, which Wor. Bro. Barnes acknowledged in a few well chosen words.

ERRATA.—On pages 19-20 of the Centennial History, issued March 1st, 1896, appears the name of "R. R. Boys." Same should read: "R. R. Boyd."

Dunn's Bicentennial History (1995)

Alton G. Dunn, Jr. ("Dunnie" to those who knew him) was initiated into Otsego Lodge in 1949 and served as Master in 1958. He served as both Historian and substitute Secretary during his Masonic career, so naturally he was designated as the appropriate member to present a history for the bicentennial celebrations in 1995. In 1996 he received a double honor from the Grand Lodge of New York, earning the Dedicated Service Award and being appointed as Grand Representative to the Grand Lodge of Missouri.

Like the 1906 update, the bicentennial history was physically no more than a paper bound pamphlet. It measures 5.5 x 8.5 inches in size, with a white paper cover. The text is set in black type and imposed upon a blue background surrounded by a decorative frame of meander and featuring an image of the "Three Great Lights" (the Holy Bible, Square, and Compasses). The fifteen pages are printed on a heavy stock and stapled. The pamphlet bears the imprint of "n.j.morrison : printing, signs & designs" (followed by an Oneonta phone exchange) on the back cover. There is no title page, page numbers, dedication or anything other than the text.

However, the pamphlet does contain a little more than what was reproduced here in this current volume. There are three main sections: a preface, the history of the lodge, and the Historian's Report for 1994, but only the final section is set off by a separate heading. The following is a list of the full contents of Dunn's presentation, including relevant short commentary (in parentheses).

- Preface (Not truly a preface, but more of an introduction to Freemasonry included for those visitors at the celebration who were not familiar with the philosophy and purpose of Masonry. The text is reproduced from a speech given on June 6, 1995 by then Otsego-Schoharie District Deputy Grand Master Duncan M. Bellinger at the presentation of the DeWitt Clinton Community Service Award to Mr. Henry J. Nichols at Otsego Lodge. This has been excluded.)
- History of Otsego Lodge, No. 138, F. & A. M., Cooperstown, N. Y. (The text is reproduced here in full with the following exceptions: a brief paragraph on early Otsego settlement and full text of the original charter reproduced elsewhere in this volume, and two paragraphs giving details of bequests to the lodge and other financial information considered private.)
- REPORT OF HISTORIAN OF OTSEGO LODGE NO. 138, F. & A.M. for the year 1994 (This has been excluded.)

As a set, the history pamphlet is accompanied by two other brochures, the dinner program and an officer's tableau. Attached to the lodge minutes are also tickets for the dinner and luncheons.

Dunn's bicentennial history was probably not intended to be more than a summary of the lodge's history, to be presented at the celebration banquet. It is frequently repetitive of what Van Horne had previously written, but does include some new information. Of special note is the added narrative regarding the secret meeting place of the lodge when it was forced underground during the "Morgan Period" in the first part of the 19th century. As a Native Son and the second of three generations to serve as Master of Otsego Lodge, Dunnie was tapped into such local legends. While the story may have originated with him, some further research may either validate or disprove his theory. I myself still repeat it as one plausible explanation of the situation until proven otherwise.

Alton G. Dunn, Jr. in one of his favorite roles as Tyler for the Masters' Investiture Ceremony of the Otsego-Schoharie Masonic District. (Bump Tavern, The Farmers' Museum, Cooperstown, 1999.)

HISTORY
OTSEGO LODGE #138

CELEBRATING 200 YEARS
AUGUST 14, 1995
1795 - 1995

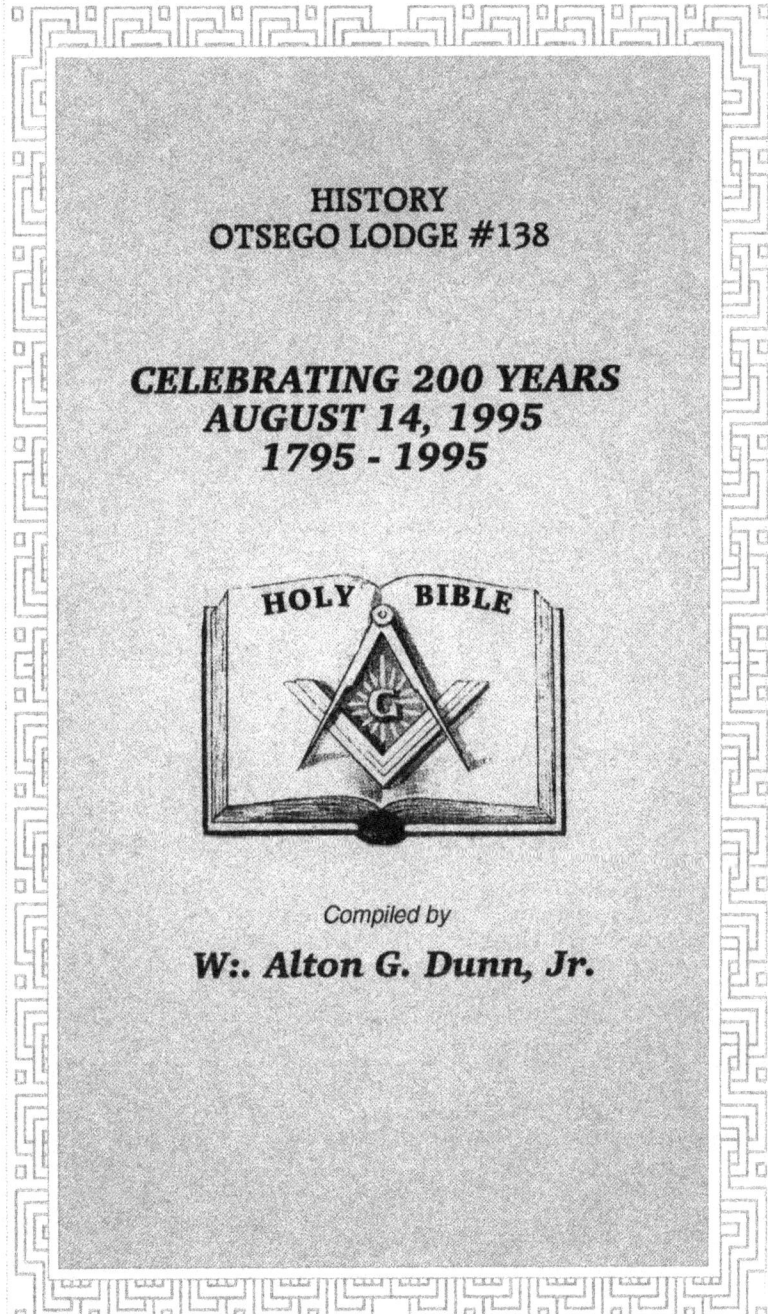

Compiled by

W:. Alton G. Dunn, Jr.

Facsimile section removed.

On September 1, 1795, a dispensation was granted to install the officers named in the Warrant, which was thereafter done in Albany. The first meeting was held on Thursday, March 1, 1796, at the home of Wor. Bro. Elihu Phinney, W.M., who appointed Bros. B. Gilbert, Treas; R. Bartlett, Secy; R. Edwards, S.D.; L. Edson, J.D.;S. Ingalls, Sr. Steward; Levi Collar, Jr. Steward; & Ezra Eaton, Tyler. Present were Bros. Gott, Tanner, Draper, and a visitor, Bro. Parker. Five names were presented as candidates for initiation. At an "Extra" Lodge the same date, Elijah Holt was balloted for, accepted, and initiated. There were 17 charter members. In 1796 there were 54 initiated and 3 affiliated. In 1797 there were 25 initiated and 1 affiliated. Otsego Lodge had the first warrant issued in the now Otsego-Schoharie Masonic District, in 1795. After the original petition (previous to April, 1795), and before the issuance of the warrant on August 14, 1795, permission needed to be obtained from the then nearest lodges, which may have included Rochester, & perhaps persons to assume the offices of master and wardens of the new lodge, reflected in the names of these persons in the original warrant.

At the first meeting, March 1, 1796, it was resolved to hold regular meetings on the first Tuesdays at 3:00 o'clock, p.m.; changed in January, 1808, to the Tuesday on or preceding the full moon, at 3 o'clock p.m.; after 1812 meetings were held at a later hour; May 13, 1862, regular meetings were changed from Tuesday to Saturday evenings; Feb. 18, 1868, the By-Laws were amended to hold meetings on the first and third Tuesdays of each month excepting June, July, and August, which should have but one meeting on the first Tuesday. Many "Extra" meetings were held in the early years, chiefly for proposing candidates and conferring degrees. For example, in August of 1803; Regular Lodge Aug. 2, 5803; committee to settle all matters of Difference between Brother C. Metcalf and Brother Averill; Resolved that the Brethren wear some badge of Mourning for Bro. S. Smith Deceased for the space of one month. Extra Lodge Aug. 2, 5803 A candidate was proposed and $2.00 deposited. Extra Lodge Aug. 8, 5803 Bro Edward proposed Andrew McCollum and Ralph Worthington as candidates for masonry; Deposits made; Resolved that Brother James Averill Junior be requested to deliver into the hands of the Worshipful Master within Ten Days from the siting of this Lodge in writing a full and accurate statement of the accusations that he has against Brother Elijah H. Metcalf unless prevented by some extraordinary accident; Resolved that the Secretary be requested to serve Brother James Averill Junior with a Copy of the foregoing resolution; Lodge closed and to stand closed until the first Tuesday of September next then to meet at this place at 5 o'clock in the p.m. unless some sudden emergency shall require its convention sooner; N.B. Brother James Averill Junior was served with a Copy of the above Resolution August 9, 5803 Benjamin Chamberlain, Secty. P.T. Extra Lodge Aug. 12, 5803 (on first step); Lodge proceeded to ballot for Andrew McCollum who was accepted and initiated. Pd Initiation fee $12; which was Pd over to Br Stacy Treas^r- Two Dollars recd last Lodge night by Br Chamberlain Pd 1 to Treas^r and 1 to Bro Eaton Tyler Pd 2.00 to Treas^r (Deposit of B Worthington). Extra Lodge Aug. 12, 5803 Lodge passed to the degree of fellow Craft; Brother Andrew McCollum being desirous to pass to the more honorable degree of a fellow Craft. who on examination was found worthy and passed accordingly; Lodge raised to the sublime degree of Master Mason Br Andrew McCollum being desirous to take the sublime Degree of a Master Mason who on examination being found worthy was raised accordingly; Lodge reduced & closed – to stand closed until the first Tuesday in September next then to meet at this place at 5 o'clock P.M. unless some sudden emergency shall require its convention sooner "For Proceedings of next regular Lodge - See three pages forward--" (minutes were apparently first on a loose sheet of paper and later transcribed into the minute book).

Meetings were held at the home of Wor. Bro. Phinney from March 1, 1796 to August 2, 1796. On August 16, 1796 meetings were changed to be held at the home of Bro. Samuel Huntington, on the South West corner of Second and West streets (now Main and Pioneer). Meetings were held at this location (the same geographical location (now 77 Main St.) as the Lodge meetings from 1920 to date, 1995), - until December 1797 when the first Masonic Hall was dedicated. Meanwhile, Bro. Huntington's house was replaced by the Eagle Hotel, which was destroyed in the great conflagration of April 12, 1862.

March 7, 1797, it was resolved "to build a Masonic Hall the ensuing season, not to exceed the expense of 300 pounds." Each brother who would contribute was to "be allowed seven per cent interest until refunded". Judge William Cooper having offered to convey the land after a satisfactory structure had been erected, a committee contracted with Bros. Sprague, Whipple and Kellogg to build the Hall on the North East corner of Front and West Streets (now Lake and Pioneer). The frame was raised June 24, 1797, and tradition relates that not a loud word was spoken upon the ground nor a metal tool used on this interesting occasion. The cornerstone was of cut limestone bearing on the face the inscription, "A.L. 5797." A copper plate 10 X 5½ X ⅛ inches was set in the top of the stone on which was inscribed in Latin:

ANNO LUCIS VMDCCXCVII DIE JUNII XXIV
HAEC AULA ERECTA FUIT, A MEMBRIS
OTSEGO SOCIETY OF LATIMORUM SOCIETATIS E. P. M.
ET DEDICATI USUI FILIORUM LUCIS.
NON NOBIS SOLUM NATI SUMUS
SED PARTIM PATRIAE PARTIM AMICIS.

The translation is about as follows: " On the 24th day of June, in the year of Light 5797, this Hall was erected by the Otsego Society of Latimorus, E.P.M., and was dedicated to the use of the Brethren of Light."
"We're born and live not to ourselves alone; But equally for country and friends of every home." An explanation of the use of the term E.P.M. may be that, until a visit of the Grand Lecturer in February, 1858, the Lodge was always opened on the Entered Apprentice Degree ("first step"). Hence it was often styled a "Lodge of Entered Apprentice Masons." the Hall was completed and dedicated December 28, 1797, on which occasion a sermon was delivered by Bro.

Ernst, Wor. Bro. Phinney composed a dedicatory song or ode which was sung. The Lodge room on the second floor, which faced East, was not carpeted until mid-Century, and the only seats were coarse benches, one row against the wall on both sides, and about two feet from them were other benches on both sides of the room, with a shelf on the back side near the top, from which the brethren took refreshments, "which in early days were never omitted, and all we had to do was to turn in our seats and face the bench, and help ourselves". Refreshments at meetings might consist of crackers, cheese, and gin, the same being provided by the stewards, who were reimbursed by the lodge on presentation of bills. Early accounts were reckoned in pounds, shillings, and pence. Senior and junior stewards were appointed each year through 1867. From 1868 on, senior and junior masters of ceremony were appointed instead of stewards, although the By-Laws of 1874 still called for stewards as officers. Masters of ceremony used stewards' staves (though not their jewels) until the latter part of the twentieth century. On June 5, 1798, Judge William Cooper presented a deed "of the land whereon the Hall now stands".

October 4, 1796, it was voted that Bro. Worshipful Elihu Phinney provide a Bible for the use of the Lodge, to the amount of seventeen dollars." At the stated communication held on January 7th, 1800, the death of our worthy and illustrious brother, General George Washington, was duly announced by Wor. Bro. Phinney, when, after reading and adopting certain resolutions passed by the Most Wor. Grand Lodge of the State of New York on this mournful occasion, resolutions of mourning for a term of six months as a tribute of respect for Gen. Washington were duly passed by the Lodge.

Otsego Lodge No. 41, F. & A.M., was incorporated in 1827 under an "Act of the Legislature of 1825", which vested in the Lodge the authority to own and hold real estate, and an insurance was placed on the property, the value of the Hall and lot being fixed at a sum not exceeding one thousand dollars. At the close of 1797 the membership had increased to one hundred three, and at the cessation of work in 1827 the total admissions numbered three hundred eighty-one. For many years the annual dues were 50 cents; Between 1860 and 1890 there were three increases, to $1.00, $1.50 and $2.00.

During the Anti-Masonic excitement which prevailed so extensively, especially in the western part of the State, it was deemed advisable to hold no meetings of the Lodge but such as were necessary to save the real estate, elect officers, etc.. Otsego Lodge, like many another lodge, came near being wrecked by the violent waves of persecution, but thanks to a few loyal Members, it was saved. The then worshipful master, E.B. Crandall; William Nichols; Kent Jarvis; Ariel Thayer; Seth Doubleday, Jr.; William Wilson; Harvey Luce; Abner Graves and few others held only one meeting a year from 1828 to 1846, with but few exceptions. At this meeting each year officers were elected and installed, and a committee was appointed to take care of the Hall and rent. From March, 1827 to September, 1846, no Work (conferring of degrees) was done. There exists with respect to this period a completely plausible and irrefutable legend bolstered by type of building construction and Masonic emblems which remained in the building known as "The Smithy" at 55 Pioneer Street, Cooperstown, a building erected in 1786 by Judge Cooper and later altered and extended. It is said that during the period of unrest described above, in spite of ownership of the "old Masonic Hall", the Masons gathered for their meetings on the top (third) floor of The Smithy, entering by a rear outside staircase perhaps to the second floor - a less visible procedure than open use of entrance to the Hall, two blocks North. There seems to be no written evidence of this practice in the Lodge records, which is understandable through 1846. A possible reason for continued secrecy is the removal of stated meetings from one building to another without dispensation or approval from Grand Lodge. In any case, the Lodge met at the old Hall in 1830 when Rt. Wor. Henry Clark, Grand Visitor, visited the Lodge and received $6.50 "in full for dues to date." No further visits were made, and no notice or call for dues was received by the Lodge. March 13th, 1832, a motion was made to sell the Hall, which was lost. A resolution was passed December 16th, 1834, to "convey by quit claim deed to Horace Baldwin two feet in front and rear of the east side of the lot now owned by the Lodge, for $35, it being understood that said Baldwin is forever to keep the line fence in good repair, and that said conveyance be made at the expense of said Baldwin."

The strong anti-Masonic excitement produced in many an apathy on the subject, the tide of emigration which swept over the country took away the young and enterprising, so that in the fall of 1846, within the radius of three miles, only nine members belonging to this Lodge could be found, including some whose infirmities were such as to prevent their attendance. In 1845, a strong desire was manifested by the Brethren to resume Labor, but it was difficult at times to get together enough members for the election of officers. At the election, December 9, 1845, it was resolved that "When this Lodge closes, it shall stand closed till the next St. John's Day (Dec. 27) at two o'clock p.m., at which time shall be installed the officers elected, and that our Brother Chaplain be requested to deliver a discourse on that occasion." The officers were duly installed on the day appointed, but Brother Potter, the Chaplain, being abroad at the time, the discourse failed. During the year, 1846, the regular meetings of the Lodge were punctually attended, but the members were aware that their condition was one of irregularity, they not having paid dues to, or held communication with, the Grand Lodge for a number of years and, as a consequence, their Warrant had become forfeitable; but such also was the condition of most other lodges in this jurisdiction, and it was expected that the Grand Lodge, on being appealed to, and "the true state of our situation laid before it, would hail our renovation with rapture, and again fold us in its fraternal embraces." During the winter of 1847 (1846-47), no work having been done for many years, the elections of the Lodge having been regularly held, the members of the Lodge supposing they were still a regularly constituted Lodge, having power to meet and work; and thus persuaded, after due consideration, it was deemed advisable to gather up the fragments. Thus with the attendance of a number of Masonic brethren who had moved into the village and vicinity, work was resumed & 16 new members were added by initiation & 11 affiliation., the Officers intending when an opportunity occurred to open communication with the Grand Lodge, if that body was still in existence, and pay such dues as that body might require. Shortly after the June communication it became known through the profane that a visitor from the Grand Lodge would soon appear and demand the Warrant. Shortly afterward the Senior Grand Warden arrived in accordance with the following extract from the minutes of the Grand Lodge:

"Grand Lodge of the State of New York,)
         Annual Meeting, June A.L. 5847.)
     Resolved, That R.W. Bro. E.S. Barnum, Senior Grand Warden, be authorized and requested to demand and receive the Warrant and property of the late Otsego Lodge, No. 41, at Cooperstown.
     Extract from the minutes. R.R. Boyd, Gd. Sec'y.:
He appeared at a regular meeting, and in the name of the Grand Lodge demanded the surrender of the Warrant. After due consideration it was decided, for the time being, to refuse, fearing that a compliance would forfeit the real estate to the State, and a compromise was finally made to stay the proceedings by referring the matter to the M.W. Grand Master. Correspondence followed, when it was ascertained that this Lodge, with many others, was stricken from the Grand Lodge list in 1839, for the non-payment of dues, a fact which was entirely unknown to the members of this Lodge. Meetings were at once discontinued, except such as were necessary for reorganizing, and a delegate was sent to confer with the Grand Lodge, who failed in making a compromise. December 21st, 1847, a committee, consisting of Bro's Seth Doubleday and James Hyde, was appointed to confer with the M. W. Grand Master, who prayed that under

the peculiar circumstances of the case, - the brethren having acted in good faith, and if errors had been committed they were unintentional - the present Warrant might be revived and continued, if, in the opinion of the Grand Lodge, it could constitutionally be done, and if not, that a new Warrant be granted as a renewal or continuance of the old one, that the real estate owned by the Lodge might be continued to it, and preserved and devoted to the Masonic purposes for which it was intended. At the annual communication of the Grand Lodge of the State of New York, in 1848, the matter of Otsego Lodge was referred to a committee, with favorable result, as the following endorsement on the old Warrant shows:

"In Grand Lodge of the State of New York, June 8th, 1848, it was Resolved, That a new Warrant be granted to Otsego Lodge No. 41 in continuance of the old Warrant, on payment of the constitutional fee.

That Ariel Thayer be named thereon as Master, James L. Fox as Senior Warden, and Eliab P. Byram, Junior Warden. and under the peculiar circumstances of the case, said Lodge is also allowed to retain its old Warrant, with an endorsement written on its face that a new Warrant has been issued in continuation thereof.

Transactions of Grand Lodge, page 55."

Across the face of the old Warrant is written:

"This Warrant having been surrendered to the Grand Lodge, a new one under the number 138 has been issued in its stead.

Otsego Lodge will hereafter work under the new Warrant, as this is no longer in force.

R.R. Boyd, Grand Sec'y."

The new Warrant, under date of June 17th, 1848, bears the seal of the Grand Lodge and the signatures of J. D. Willard, Grand Master; Oscar Coles, Deputy Grand Master; Ezra S. Barnum, Junior Grand Warden, and R. R. Boyd, Grand Sec'y. With the above named Warrant and forty-four members labor was resumed as Otsego Lodge No. 138, F. & A. M..

Election of Officers had been held December 21, 1847. June 20, 1848, an informal meeting saw appointment of a committee to direct and superintend needful repairs to the Hall and property, $100.00 being expended. By-Laws were revised and prepared for adoption when it might legally be done. August 8, 1848, the officers elected Dec. 21, 1847, were installed under the name and style of Otsego Lodge No. 138. June 2, 1849, proposed amendments to the Grand Lodge Constitution were submitted to Otsego Lodge No. 138, approved, and their adoption recommended. Soon after 1850 the lodge room was carpeted and new furniture added throughout. The foundation was also relaid.

From its inception to 1827, and after 1847 for many years,

elaborate observances were held to celebrate the Festivals of St. John the Evangelist and St. John the Baptist, in December and June, usually by a sermon at one of the village churches, followed by a dinner and program at the Lodge Room or a local hotel. The lodge gathered for participation in local church service at other times, sometimes for service conducted by a Reverend Brother, and other times by the applicable clergyman not a Mason. This practice, continuing with declining frequency through the first half of the twentieth century, has been discontinued in the last several decades.

In 1865, "for the better accommodation of the fraternity", rooms were rented in the "Phinney Block" on the East side of Pioneer Street, at one hundred dollars a year, and the old Hall abandoned for Lodge purposes. From 1850 for several decades the Lodge enjoyed a good relationship with Otsego Lodge No. 106, I.O. of Odd Fellows, including attendance, jointly at several funerals. In 1882, by consent of the W.W. Grand Master, communications were held at Odd Fellows Hall on Main Street while the Phinney Block was undergoing repairs. In 1871, the Lodge concurred with Otsego Chapter No. 26, R.A.M., to permit Otsego Council, R. & S.M. to hold their meetings in the Hall, free of rent, they paying their just proportion of bill for fuel and gas, until they were financially able to pay rent. In 1877, a large double lot in Lakewood Cemetery was purchased for Masonic burials. Several masons have been buried there, including at least one sojourner. Several expenditures have been authorized from time to time for refurbishing gravestones of Masons at this and other locations. In June 1880, after elaborate preparations, several hundred masons participated in a parade and the laying of the cornerstone for the new County court House.

The Phinney Block was purchased by the Lodge in 1886 for $5,500.00 and the old Hall at 30 Lake Street was sold for $2,000.00. the old Hall on Lake Street was first lighted by gas in 1861. the Phinney Block was first lighted by electricity in 1888. The present building at 77 Main Street (and lot 80' X 44½') was purchased in 1920 for $19,000.00 to include cost of necessary renovations. This mortgage was discharged in December 1941 when a deed was recorded to the lodge covering premises at the rear of the lot (44½' X 7'), and a new mortgage for $17,000.00 was given to Second National Bank of Cooperstown, which mortgage was discharged of record December 4, 1963.

October, 1805, a petition for a warrant from brethren at Richfield was "laid on the table". No further action was shown. January, 1806, a similar petition from Cherry Valley brethren was recommended "provided the officers named meet the approval of the members". In 1816 the lodge again voted to approve a petition of Cherry Valley. Petitions for warrants for Milford were denied in 1812 and 1815, but approved in 1826. Petitions for warrants for Oaksville were refused in 1823 and 1824. November 22, 1825, a petition was presented for consent to remove Otsego Lodge to Oaksville. January 1824 a warrant was recommended in the town of Middlefield. In 1888 a member of Otsego Lodge referred to a lodge formerly existing at Clarksville (Middlefield). In 1855 the Lodge recommended a petition for a new Lodge at Richmondville. In 1865 consent was given to establish a new lodge at Schenevus. In 1884 about 40 members of Otsego Lodge attended the laying of cornerstone at Schenevus Lodge. In 1885 we attended laying of the cornerstone of the new State Armory at Oneonta. May 21st, 1891, a number of brethren attended the laying of the cornerstone of the Masonic Home at Utica, which was the largest assemblage of Masons ever seen in New York State.

The Masonic Home in Utica as it has grown and expanded, now including the Masonic Medica Research Laboratory, has been the largest recipient of contributions of the members of Otsego Lodge No. 138, F. & A.M., individually and collectively. We have sponsored several of our members, wives, and widows as residents there. We have also sponsored several youths as campers at Camp Turk at Round Lake in the Adirondacks - including two in 1994 and three in 1995.

A destructive fire broke out in the Masonic Block, starting in the section rented by Ellsworth & Sill, dry goods, in the early morning of Monday, February 24, 1941. Considerable damage resulted in extensive repairs and renovations to the second and third floor areas used by the Masonic bodies, as well as the portions used by tenants Ellsworth & Sill, Church & Scott, druggists, and Cooke & Basinger, attorneys. Ellsworth & Sill and Church & Scott are still our tenants; R.S. Donnelly, dentist, has succeeded Dr. E.T. Farmer, dentist, successor to some of the space used by Cooke & Basinger, attorneys.

Facsimile section removed.

At various times, Otsego Lodge has had over 300 members, including as late a period as the 1960's. At roll-call night in October, 1958, some 133 members joined by several visitors were served by the ladies of the Eastern Star in the second floor dining area, and repaired to the lodge room for a tiled meeting. Membership has recently been 106; is now 111, and five await the F.C. degree; one awaits the M.M. degree; and several have presented petitions, expecting the E.A. degree in the fall.

It seems that we are fiscally secure. If we are to have members to enjoy the facilities in the future, we must continue the present increase in membership and instill in our new members a strong feeling for the value of the teachings of Masonry, and the desire and ability to transmit them to future generations of Masons. otherwise we may some day have a fine facility and a fine altar with no one to display the great lights thereon. We close this presentation with a copy of the lodge historian's report submitted January 1995.

The annex to "The Smithy" building on Pioneer Street which bears Masonic symbols set into the stonework and the date "1826".

The Masonic symbols in the stonework of The Smithy annex.

History of Otsego Lodge Buildings

This piece has been presented in various formats at different lodge events since 2000. It was printed for oral presentations and deposited in the lodge archives, but never published until a newer version appeared in The Freeman's Journal *in August 2007. It has been updated from new research and expanded (even since then) to include more detail, combining and reconciling the information contained in the previous histories, and creating a more chronological approach. This version focuses specifically on lodge buildings and other public structures around Cooperstown which were the location of Masonic events or related in some other way to Masonic activities.*

The history of Otsego Lodge began with the arrival of Elihu Phinney. The newspaper publisher was already a Freemason when he came to Cooperstown in February of 1795—but he wasn't the first. Freemasons arrived on the shores of Lake Otsego even before William Cooper himself.

Colonel George Croghan came to America in 1741 and quickly earned a reputation as an Indian trader, mastering several tribal languages. By 1756 he had become Deputy Superintendent of Indian Affairs under his friend Sir William Johnson. In 1767, he was raised to the degree of Master Mason in St. Patrick's Lodge in Johnstown, New York. Through ruthless land speculation with the Iroquois and his influence with fellow Masons Johnson and William Franklin, he came to possess the Patent for the land which encompassed nearly all of the future Otsego County. He surveyed the land around Otsego Lake in 1768, building an elaborate residential cabin and a handful of other structures near the mouth of the Susquehanna River a year later. Unfortunately, his plans quickly crumbled and he had to flee his debtors. Croghan's activities are memorialized on Main Street with a state historical marker.

Two other Masons are remembered by markers and monuments in this location as well: General James Clinton and General John Sullivan, famous for building and exploding their dam to facilitate their military campaign down the Susquehanna. Their two main adversaries, Sir John Johnson and Chief Joseph Brant, were also Freemasons.

When Phinney arrived, he immediately began corresponding with Peter Yates of Albany, who presented his case to the Grand Lodge of the State of New York to form a lodge in Cooperstown. Since the founding Masons were gathered from the areas in and around the village, the Grand Lodge issued a charter on August 14, 1795 for the new Otsego Lodge No. 40. On December 31 of that year, Phinney and several other members (as well as those from another new lodge recently chartered in Schoharie) met at McGourk's Tavern in Albany to be installed as the newly elected officers. The lodge archives contains Phinney's copies of the original correspondence that passed between him and Yates, dating back to April 1795.

On March 1, 1796, the first meeting of Otsego Lodge was held at Phinney's home on Second Street (now Main Street). Later that year, Bro. Samuel Huntington purchased the Red Lion Tavern from Joseph Griffin, which was located at the southwest corner of Second and West streets (now Main and Pioneer).

Beginning in August and for more than a year following, the meetings were held at this location—known today as 77 Main Street—exactly where the lodge meets today.

In May of 1797, a lodge committee signed a contract with Brothers Sprague, Whipple and Kellogg for 300 pounds to build a new Masonic Hall. Another committee soon selected a building lot on the northeast corner of Front and West streets (now Lake and Pioneer). The land was to be donated by Judge Cooper after a suitable building was erected.

On June 24, 1797, the members of the lodge and visiting Brothers laid the cornerstone and erected the 22' x 44' x 22' frame of the new hall. At the conclusion of their labor, they repaired to the tavern lodge room to dine, presenting Masonic toasts under a bower of seven arches.

The cornerstone laid that day is truly a puzzle. It was cut from limestone, upon the face of which is chiseled, "A. L. 5797". A rectangular depression on the top served as a receptacle for a copper plate, which Phinney had engraved with a Latin inscription:

ANNO LUCIS, VM,DCCXCVII, DIE JUNII, XXIV.
HÆC AULA ERECTA FUIT, A MEMBRIS
OTSEGO LATAMORUM SOCIETATIS, E. P. M.
ET DEDICATA USUI FILIORUM LUCIS.

NON NOBIS SOLUM NATI SUMUS:
SED PARTIM PATRIÆ, PARTIM AMICIS.

*[On the 24th day of June, in the Year of Light 5797,
this Hall was erected by
the Otsego Society of Latimorus, E.P.M.,
and was dedicated to the use of the Brethren of Light.*

*We're born and live not to ourselves alone,
but equally for country and friends of every home.*

The translation of this has been passed down from Albert T. Van Horne, and I believe it is an incorrect translation, partly based on inaccurate transcriptions of the actual text on the plate. (See page 11 for Van Horne's discussion.) However, Van Horne was not alone in his error, for even in his own coverage of the event in *The Otsego Herald*, Phinney prints a different version of the Latin text, including a different layout and even different words! (Perhaps, like all authors and editors, he was still revising even after publication.) The Latin text above is taken directly from the plate, and retains all the layout, capitalization and punctuation as engraved. (See photo on page 38.)

I'm not sure where Van Horne picked up the word "home" or how his logic worked out the meaning behind "E.P.M.", but I think both were just pure guesswork on his part. I believe the correct meaning of the three letters is simple: "*Elihu Phinney Master*". Many cornerstones and other commemorative plaques bear the name of the head of the organization building the structure, so why not Phinney? Even in Latin it works, for either *"magister"* or *"magus"* (for "Master") works with the letters.

As for Van Horne's translation, I think the first paragraph is relatively accurate. The second paragraph requires a little more work. In my opinion, the translation of the whole stanza depends on the meaning of the word *"solum"*, which Van Horne took to mean "alone" (as in "solo"). In Latin, however, it can also mean "foundation" – a fitting interpretation considering the building was raised and born on that date. I believe a more literal (and possibly more accurate) translation, with wiggle room, to be something like *"a foundation born to exist not for us, but partly for country and partly for fellowship."* I welcome the efforts of any Latin scholars willing to take a crack at this.

On Dec. 28, 1797 the completed Masonic Hall was dedicated with Masonic ceremonies, and the members proceeded to the Cooperstown Academy where they held a great festive celebration, including an oration by Cooperstown's newest (and quickly ousted) minister, the Reverend Brother John Frederick Ernst. The following June, Judge Cooper presented the deed for the land as promised. Both this document and the building contract are held in the archives.

The lodge room had bare wooden floors and the walls were lined with two rows of wooden benches. A festive board stood directly behind those, where cheese, crackers and gin were available to the Brothers when the lodge was at refreshment. Not much else is known about the interior of the building or the furnishings.

The lodge rented the lower rooms to individual tenants over the next several decades, beginning with Rev. Benjamin Wright, immediately following the building's completion. Part of his rent was to provide firewood and candles for the lodge meetings. Fraternal tenants of the building included Otsego Mark Masters' Lodge No. 5, which was dissolved into Otsego Chapter No. 26, Royal Arch Masons, in 1809. At that time, the chapter members were allowed to renovate some of the lodge space for their own purposes, including storage areas for ritual paraphernalia.

Otsego Lodge No. 40 met at the original hall until June 4, 1819, when in a numerical rearrangement by the Grand Secretary, the lodge's charter was reissued, to then be recognized as Otsego Lodge No. 41.

Beginning in 1825 and for approximately the next two decades, the lodge experienced a period of unrest and mystery. For reasons that are unclear at this time, a petition was presented in 1825 to move the lodge to Oaksville. Perhaps this was the result of two other failed petitions in 1823 and 1824 to establish a new lodge there, the proposal being simply the act of frustrated members. But, this could also have been due to a general feeling of nervousness. For about a decade, anti-Masonic sentiment had been growing within New York State over the influence of Freemasons in the state government and the building and operation of the Erie Canal. It might be possible that certain Brothers thought it best to move the lodge out of the village and away from public concern. Whatever their reason, it soon proved irrelevant as the public's smoldering anti-Masonic feelings erupted into flame over the Morgan affair, and Otsego Lodge retreated into secrecy.

Masonic history refers to these subsequent years as "the Morgan Period." Shady events surround the abduction of one William Morgan, a self-styled "Captain" and alleged Freemason who announced the publication of a forthcoming exposé of Masonic rituals. His disappearance in 1826 and alleged murder by fellow Masons sparked outrage and was followed by a fervent period of anti-Masonic persecution.

Regardless of the fact that Morgan's fate was never proven either way, like many lodges around New York State, Otsego Lodge was severely affected and felt the need to go underground. At that time several Brothers petitioned the Master to surrender the charter to appease public opinion, but he remained faithful and held his ground. By 1828 it seemed advisable for the Brothers to hold meetings only once per year to save the real estate, elect officers, and preserve the existence of the lodge in general. With the exception of a brief attempt in 1835 to resume regular meetings, the lodge existed in this state until 1845. No degrees were conferred during this period.

Otsego Lodge's meeting minutes during the Morgan Period reflect this strategy as they were faithfully recorded once per year, but they never state where the meetings were held, as usual. Presumably the members did not meet in open view at the Masonic Hall. A possible reason for the lack of documentation is the removal of lodge meetings from one building to another without the approval of the Grand Lodge.

According to former Otsego Lodge historian Alton G. Dunn, Jr. and former Grand Historian Wilmer E. Bresee (of Oneonta Lodge No. 466), the prevailing legend says that the members met in secret on one of the upper floors of the extension of the building known as "The Smithy," built in 1786 by Judge Cooper and later altered and extended. (The annex, now a separate building, stands today at 51 Pioneer Street.) The legend is bolstered by the fact of the curious symbols set into the stonework of the front façade. Still clearly visible, the stones depict the familiar square and compasses symbol, a pillar, and a lodge Master in a top hat.

Probably of more importance to the legend than the symbols is the number "1826" set into the stonework. One has to stand directly in front to distinguish the numbers, but they are definitely there. This date, of course, is the year that William Morgan disappeared. It is hard to decide whether this validates the theory or just creates more puzzles.

Whatever the case, the only recorded exception in the minute book is 1830, when the lodge met at the old Hall to receive a Grand Lodge representative and pay full dues to date. Probably the lodge was warned through official correspondence in advance. No further visitors from Grand Lodge were entertained during this period, and no notice or call for dues was received by the lodge. At the 1832 meeting a motion was made to sell the Hall, which was defeated. In 1834, a sliver of the plot around the east side and front of the Hall was ceded to a neighbor, who was charged with keeping the fence in good repair.

Otsego Lodge lost all communication with the Grand Lodge and existed in Masonic limbo until 1845, when the handful of remaining members decided to gather up the fragments and begin rebuilding in earnest. This action may have been inspired by the realization that the lodge was about to reach its 50th anniversary. The meetings were punctually attended by the existing members, only to receive a visit from the Senior Grand Warden in 1847, who demanded the surrender of the lodge's warrant. Unknown to Otsego Lodge, the charter, along with that of several other lodges, had been stricken from the Grand Lodge rolls in 1839 for non-payment of dues. However, after much negotiation an appeal was made to the Grand Master, and a new warrant for the lodge was issued on June 17, 1848, henceforth to be known as Otsego Lodge No. 138.

The old Masonic Hall had suffered from neglect, and just three days later a committee was formed to spend $100 to make sufficient repairs. The lodge had rented the hall to the Independent Order of Rechabites in 1845, probably as a way to generate some income for a possible rebirth and to stave off foreclosure. In 1852 the steadily recovering lodge made more repairs to the building. At that time the original cornerstone was discovered and re-laid. By 1861, the hall was being lit by gas, and Phinney's "Brotherhood of Light" was prosperous once again.

Otsego Lodge continued to meet at the original hall until 1865, when membership levels required larger quarters. Rooms were rented at the Phinney Block on the east side of Pioneer Street, just off Main. The old hall was then abandoned for lodge purposes and the entire building rented to various tenants.

In 1882, by consent of the Grand Master, the lodge moved its meetings to the hall of the Independent Order of Odd Fellows on Main Street, while repairs were being made to the Phinney Block building. Apparently the building was a suitable location, as just three years later the lodge and the Royal Arch chapter joined forces to refurbish the lodge rooms at a cost of $800.

To dedicate the new facilities, a public celebration was held, and the newspapers raved about the building. Highlights included items still on display today: a set of three paintings from 1857 depicting the symbols of the three Masonic Degrees, and the cornerstone from the original hall, complete with the copper dedication plate of Brother Phinney.

These artifacts were removed to the rented rooms in anticipation of a future property transaction, which finally took place in 1886, when the lodge purchased the Phinney Block for $5,500. The old Masonic Hall was sold to Thomas Murphy for $2,500, and has been used as a private residence ever since. It is impressive that the old wooden-framed building has withstood the test of time.

The Masonic bodies in the Phinney Block continued to improve it over the next thirty years. The building was first lit by electricity in 1888. The old organ in the lodge room was replaced with a modern model in 1899. A banquet space to accommodate 50 people was installed that same year. 1906 saw the introduction of steam heat.

The heat was installed to make the lower floor more comfortable, which housed the Post Office boxes. The lodge had purchased the boxes in 1901 and leased them back to the Postal Department under a five year lease. By 1906, "modern" mail delivery systems required a complete refurbishing and rearrangement of the space, which the lodge did at the expense of $2,000. A new lease of ten years was signed. Obviously the Post Office went elsewhere at the end of the lease, for in 1917, the lodge offered the rooms on the first floor to the Red Cross for the use of their war efforts.

Otsego Lodge continued to flourish, and as World War I started the lodge once again sensed the need for larger quarters and formed a Building Committee. In 1918 the lodge sold the Phinney Block to the Cooperstown Chamber of Commerce for $5,000. While the committee searched for a new building to occupy, the lodge rented the top two floors for their meetings. Finally, in 1920, the members voted to purchase the Bunyan Block for $19,000, which Otsego Lodge has owned and occupied ever since.

The Bunyan Block was designed as apartments and storefronts by Edward Clark's favorite architect, Henry Janeway Hardenbergh, who was commissioned to build The Dakota building in Manhattan for the sewing machine magnate. Besides the building which became the future Otsego Lodge hall, Hardenbergh also left his mark on the landscape around Otsego Lake, Kingfisher Tower and The Inn at Cooperstown being two of his more striking structures.

The top two floors of 77 Main Street were then renovated into appropriate lodge rooms, and on display today is an original drawing of the proposed layout of the third floor. One beautiful feature is the current library space, which contains a set of ornately-carved shelves. The shelves were first installed in the pharmacy of Church & Scott, who have been tenants of the building for decades.

In February 1941, a destructive fire broke out in Ellsworth & Sill, which caused extensive damage to the areas occupied by Church & Scott, and to the second and third floors used by the Masonic bodies. Past Master Perry Houghtaling, a long-standing member of both the lodge and the Cooperstown Fire Department, often recalled looking down through a hole in the floor to the other rooms below. But, even this catastrophe did not dampen the spirits of the brothers, as the necessary repairs were made, and the original mortgage on the building was paid off in December of 1941.

The lodge rooms, wherever located, have always been occupied by the affiliated Masonic bodies. Otsego Chapter No. 26, Royal Arch Masons have shared the lodge rooms since 1809. As an enduring gift of brotherhood, the chapter purchased the beautiful pipe organ which now resides in the lodge room. In 1922, Otsego Commandery No. 76, Knights Templar, was formed and began meeting in the lodge. You can see many beautiful swords, chapeaux, caps and jewels on display from this commandery and the many others who have merged with them over the years, including a mannequin dressed in an impressive Knight Templar uniform of the early 20th century, all displayed in the Club Room.

The mannequin was donated by Mrs. Joan Clark who, along with her late husband, ran a clothing store on Main Street in the "Ironclad" building. It stood in the store's front window for many years and was rescued from the basement. Its removal certainly raised the eyebrows of the usual park bench residents when a naked man was seen being carried across Main Street and into the lodge building!

The Templar mannequin has begun to take on its own aura of legend. The current members have nicknamed the statue "George" after George Harrison, a prominent member of the lodge and the commandery. Toward the end of his life, serving as a lodge trustee and historian, it seemed that George was always in the building, and would often surprise people who didn't know he was there. Now, when members open the door to enter the Club Room, they are quite startled to find a person standing in the room—only to recover and say, "Oh, George, it's only you."

Otsego-Hartwick-Arbutus Chapter No. 201, Order of the Eastern Star, celebrated its first 100 years of existence in 2000. The Chapter has contributed greatly to the lodge facilities as well, including purchasing the folding chairs and the beautiful dinnerware used for social occasions. In addition, they have contributed two wonderful pieces of fraternal folk art—a hooked rug bearing the OES emblem and a crocheted American flag which hangs in the dining room.

In the 1990s the building suffered water damage, beginning with strong winds which blew away the tarps installed during the replacement of the roof and sent heavy rains into the building, literally soaking the third floor. Luckily, insurance paid for the damage, and the lodge became inspired to begin preserving the history of the lodge in earnest. Plans were made to renovate the Club Room on the second floor into an artifact showroom. Past Master William Cernik, who played a major part in these efforts, did a meticulous and beautiful job restoring and painting the tin ceilings, radiators and light sconces. New furniture was purchased and the old billiards table donated away.

Around Cooperstown, the lodge has made use of or contributed to the recognition of certain structures as well. Twice the cornerstones of the Otsego County buildings have been laid with Masonic ceremonies. First, the County Court House on June 15, 1880, and again the County Clerk's building on July 28, 1900. The court house cornerstone is still in place, and the cornerstone of the old clerk's building was saved and rests among the landscaping in the promenade to the new County Office building.

A new tradition of Masonic use of county facilities was started early in this decade when Otsego Lodge received dispensation from the Grand Master to hold a regular meeting at the county nursing home. Since Past Masters Arthur Jenkins, Jr. and Perry R. Hotaling were members who could no longer make it to the lodge, the members went to them and set up a makeshift lodge in the chapel. Other Masons from around the Otsego-Schoharie Masonic District often join them to renew the bonds of fellowship.

Before the lodge installed the dining hall in the Phinney Block in 1899, they usually held dinners for celebrations at many of the village's larger spaces. Among them have been Academy Hall, the Fireman's Hall, the Central Hotel and the Hotel Fenimore, all of which are long since gone. Van Horne describes many of these events in detail. Event though today the lodge in the Bunyan Block has a large dining room that is often filled to capacity for events, twice in the 1990's the lodge celebrated events with a banquet at The Otesaga Hotel, including the lodge bicentennial in 1995.

Otsego Lodge has held many funerals at Lakewood Cemetery, where it purchased a plot around 1878. The funerals have not only been for its members, but for other Masons as well. A notable example is James McNally who, as a member of Eastern Star Lodge No. 227, died in Cooperstown and was buried with Masonic services performed by Otsego Lodge. Van Horne describes the event and the beautiful testimonial certificate presented to the Cooperstown Brethren on page 29. Otsego

Lodge has also contributed to the restoration of various Masonic gravestones, many of which can be seen scattered around Cooperstown's graveyards displaying the familiar square and compasses symbol. As part of the lodge's bicentennial celebration in 1995, the members placed a commemorative plaque on the exterior of the original hall, and another marker next to Elihu Phinney's grave in Lakewood Cemetery.

In addition to Masonic funeral services, Otsego Lodge has gathered many times over the years at the local houses of worship. Van Horne's writings and the lodge archives are filled with information about church-related events, including joint services with other organizations, calls to prayer during wartime, and public observances and orations on the Masonic "holy days" of St. John the Baptist and St. John the Evangelist. In 1826, Otsego Lodge helped to lay a cornerstone adorned with Masonic symbols for the Baptist church in the nearby community of Middlefield.

Otsego Lodge has also made frequent use of the historic buildings at The Farmers Museum. In 1987, a Masonic lodge exhibit was established in a small room above the print shop. Lodge furniture and artifacts were requested from and loaned by several lodges around the state, and a lodge room reflecting the post-Morgan Period was set up for all visitors to see.

Many members recall with fondness their visit to the austere but beautiful lodge room. However, this lodge exhibit could only be accessed by a small flight of stairs, and these proved to be the exhibit's downfall. Fearing for the safety of visitors and concerned over it's accessibility by elderly members, The Farmers' Museum closed the exhibit in 1997. Within the past year, the artifacts were all safely returned to the appropriate lodge owners. In many cases, items were delivered directly to the lodges through the generosity of the museum.

After the exhibit closed, the Brothers who lived in Cooperstown and the Otsego-Schoharie District still wanted to see a Masonic presence at the museum. Fraternal societies were an important part of the fabric of village life in upstate New York. It was recognized at that time that Masons once met in "Bump Tavern," a building which was moved from Greene County and erected on the grounds of the museum. The members and Katie Boardman, an employee of the museum and a specialist in 19th-century fraternal orders, sought to re-establish a Masonic presence by creating a "traveling lodge" exhibit on the upper floor of the tavern, which opened in 1999.

The exhibit consisted of a chest filled with the furniture necessary to set up a temporary lodge room, as was done in the heyday of the tavern itself. The chest was reproduced by the museum from an artifact held at The National Heritage Museum in Lexington, Massachusetts. Along with the ritual paraphernalia, there were laminated images culled from various books on Masonry depicting famous Masons, symbolic paintings and other Masonic artifacts. It was set up on weekends when individual Masons from the area were on hand to volunteer as exhibit interpreters. In addition, Erik Strohl, Past Master of Otsego Lodge in Cooperstown, wrote and presented an interpretation of the exhibit as part of his class work as a student in the Cooperstown Graduate Program in Museum Studies. His interpretation was used as guide for the volunteer docents. Unfortunately, the traveling lodge exhibit has since been discontinued as well. All the items in the replica chest have been returned or turned over to The Chancellor Robert R Livingston Masonic Library of Grand Lodge, along with photos of the original exhibit and other documentation.

At the same time as the opening of the Bump Tavern exhibit, the Brothers of the Otsego-Schoharie and Delaware Masonic Districts began to hold their annual Master's Investiture Ceremony in the tavern. At the first event, Ms. Boardman handed out copies of old Masonic songs and accompanied a chorus of Brothers on a melodeon, a vintage portable keyboard driven by foot pedals. Together they recorded a couple of old tunes. That enjoyable evening set the precedent for the future, and the May event has been attended by either a Grand Master or Deputy Grand Master every year since.

If you believe the legend that the lodge met in secret at The Smithy, then you could consider it ironic that a few years ago the lodge presented a very public history exhibit in one of the galleries now located there. Entitled "Freemasonry in Cooperstown: The Embodiment of Community Service," the display focused on Freemasonry's role in the community and featured many artifacts from the lodge, as well as the photos and stories of members who were prominent in both lodge and local affairs. The exhibit panels themselves are now used for displays at lodge events, such as the Open House held for the Village Bicentennial in 2007.

A history of Otsego Lodge buildings would not be complete without mentioning the Trustees. These Brothers, three of whom are elected for three-year terms annually, are charged with the oversight of the lodge buildings, wherever they have been located. To those Brothers we owe the thanks of the lodge and the community.

Original Otsego Lodge hall, erected in 1797 and still at Lake and Pioneer Streets.

The Phinney Block on Pioneer Street, home to Otsego Lodge from 1865 to 1920.

The Bunyan Block on Main and Pioneer Streets, designed by Henry J. Hardenbergh. Otsego Lodge purchased the building in 1920 and has remained there since.

Charters of Otsego Lodge

The original charter or warrant of Otsego Lodge No. 40 is still in the lodge's possession. Van Horne quoted both the original and the new charters in his centennial history (and which was later copied by Dunn) but he was not entirely accurate. The texts presented here were taken directly from the primary documents. The spellings, capitalizations, emphasis and paragraph formatting have been reproduced as closely as possible.

The following is from the original warrant:

WE, THE GRAND LODGE of the most Ancient and Honourable Fraternity of FREE AND ACCEPTED MASONS, of the STATE OF NEW YORK, in ample form assembled, according to the Old Constitutions regularly and solemnly established under the Auspices of PRINCE EDWIN, at the City of York, in Great Britain, in the year of Masonry, 4926, viz.

> The Most Worshipful The Honorable Robert R. Livingston, Esquire, Chancellor of the State, GRAND MASTER.
> The Right Worshipful Jacob Morton, Esquire, DEPUTY GRAND MASTER.
> The Right Worshipful James Scott, Esquire, SENIOR GRAND WARDEN.
> The Right Worshipful Dewitt Clinton, Esquire, JUNIOR GRAND WARDEN.

DO by these Presents, appoint, authorize and empower our worthy Brother Elihu Phinney to be the Master, our worthy Brother Rowland Cotton to be the Senior Warden, and our worthy Brother James Fitch to be the Junior Warden, of a Lodge of Free and Accepted Masons, to be, by virtue hereof constituted, formed and held at Cooperstown, in the county of Otsego and State of New York, which Lodge shall be distinguished by the Name or Title of Otsego Lodge No. 40, and the said Master and Wardens, and their successors in Office, are hereby respectively authorised and directed, by and with the Assistance and Consent of a Majority of the Members of said LODGE, duly to be summoned and present upon such Occasions, to ELECT AND INSTALL the Officers of the said LODGE as Vacancies happen, in Manner and Form as is or may be prescribed by the CONSTITUTION, of this GRAND LODGE.-------AND FURTHER, the said Lodge is hereby invested with full Power and Authority to assemble upon proper and lawful Occasions, and to MAKE MASONS-----to ADMIT MEMBERS,---as also to do and perform all and every such Acts and Things appertaining to the CRAFT as have been, and ought to be done, for the Honour and Advantage thereof; conforming in all their proceedings to the CONSTITUTIONS of this GRAND LODGE, otherwise this warrant and the Powers thereby granted to cease and be of no further effect.

GIVEN under our Hands and the Seal of our GRAND LODGE, in the City of New York, in North America, this fourteenth day of August, in the year of our LORD One Thousand Seven Hundred, and ninety-five, and in the Year of our MASONRY, Five Thousand Seven Hundred, and ninety-five.

John Abrams, Grand Secretary.

When the lodge was renumbered as Otsego Lodge No. 41, an endorsement was written on the reverse of the original charter, the text apparently copied from the *Proceedings of the Grand Lodge* for the year 1819, page 40:

In Grand Lodge of the State of New York, June 4, 1819, pursuant to the numerical arrangement submitted by the Grand Secretary, it was

> Ordered, that Otsego Lodge, held at Cooperstown, hitherto known as No. 40, be hereafter stiled No. 41.

Following the Morgan Period and the negotiations with the Grand Lodge over the validity of the charter, the lodge was allowed to continue. A further endorsement was written on the back of the original warrant, the text apparently copied from the *Transactions of the Grand Lodge* for the year 1848, page 55:

In Grand Lodge of the State of New York, June 8, 1848, it was

> Resolved, That a new Warrant be granted to Otsego Lodge No. 41 in continuance of the Old Warrant, on payment of the constitutional fee. That Ariel Thayer be named thereon as Master, James L. Fox as S. W., and Eliab P. Byram, J. W. And under the peculiar circumstances of the case, said Lodge is also allowed to retain its Old Warrant, with an endorsement written on its face that a new Warrant has been issued in continuation thereof.

When the lodge was reconstituted that final endorsement was written across the front of the original charter:

This warrant having been surrendered to the Grand Lodge, a new one under the number 138 has been issued in its stead. Otsego Lodge will hereafter work under the new Warrant, as this one is no longer in effect.

R. R. Boyd, Gr Sec.

The lodge retains its current charter as Otsego Lodge No. 138, which must be present at every meeting of the lodge. The text of the document follows.

WE, THE GRAND LODGE of the Most Ancient and Honourable Fraternity of FREE AND ACCEPTED MASONS of the STATE OF NEW YORK, in ample Form assembled, according to the Old Constitutions regularly and solemnly established under the Auspices of PRINCE EDWIN, at the City of York, in Great Britain, in the Year of masonry 4926, viz.

THE MOST WORSHIPFUL the Hon. John D. Willard of Troy GRAND MASTER.
THE RIGHT WORSHIPFUL Oscar Coles, Esq. City of New York DEPUTY GRAND MASTER.
THE RIGHT WORSHIPFUL Richard Carrique, Esq. of Hudson SENIOR GRAND WARDEN.
THE RIGHT WORSHIPFUL Ezra S. Barnum, Esq. of Utica JUNIOR GRAND WARDEN.

DO by these Presents, appoint, authorise and empower our worthy Brother Ariel Thayer to be the Master; our worthy Brother James L. Fox to be the Senior Warden; and our worthy Brother Eliab P. Byrum to be the Junior Warden, of a Lodge of FREE AND ACCEPTED MASONS, to be, by Virtue hereof, constituted, formed and held in Cooperstown in the county of Otsego in this state which Lodge shall be distinguished by the Name and Style of Otsego Lodge No. 138 and the said Master and Wardens, and their successors in Office, are hereby respectively authorised and directed, by and with the Assistance and Consent of a Majority of the Members of said LODGE, duly to be summoned and present upon such Occasions, to ELECT and INSTALL the Officers of the said Lodge as Vacancies happen, in manner and form as is, or may be, prescribed by the CONSTITUTION of this GRAND LODGE.--------AND FURTHER, the said Lodge is hereby invested with full Power and Authority to assemble upon proper and lawful Occasions, and to MAKE MASONS-----to ADMIT MEMBERS-----as also to do and perform all and every such Acts and Things appertaining to the CRAFT as have been, and ought to be done, for the Honour and Advantage thereof; conforming in all their Proceedings to the CONSTITUTIONS of this GRAND LODGE, otherwise this WARRANT and the Powers thereby granted to cease and be of no further Effect.

GIVEN under our Hands and the Seal of our GRAND LODGE, in the City of New York, United States of America, this 17th day of June, in the year of our Lord, One Thousand Eight Hundred and forty eight, and in the Year of our MASONRY, Five Thousand Eight Hundred and forty eight,

R. R. Boyd, Grand Secretary.

Elihu Phinney
Printer & Newspaper Publisher
First Worshipful Master of Otsego Lodge
Founder of Freemasonry in Cooperstown

Masters of Otsego Lodge

The election to the office of Master in Otsego Lodge is a procedure regulated by the Grand Lodge of the State of New York and the By-Laws of the lodge. The five principal officers (Master, Senior and Junior Wardens, Secretary and Treasurer) are elected annually by the members of the lodge. A secret ballot is conducted in a stated lodge meeting using a ballot box containing white balls and black cubes or black balls. A white ball is a positive vote; a black cube or black ball is a negative vote (from which the notorious term derives). Other subordinate officers are appointed by the Master to serve for the ensuing year, and generally each year the members simply "step up" an office, culminating in being elected as Master. Following a very active year in his life, that member simply steps down and once again becomes a regular member (unless elected or appointed to another office, such as Secretary). However, serving just a single year as Master has not always been the case.

Beginning with Elihu Phinney serving as the first Master of Otsego Lodge in 1796, there have been a total of 212 sitting Masters, one for each year. There have been 127 different Masters during that time. Of those, 91 served just one year. The reasons for this vary (including doing a poor job), but usually this happens because there are enough new members in the line of officers that every member who so desires can eventually serve as Master.

25 men have served twice as Master of Otsego Lodge. As with those who served only once, circumstances dictate the reasons: they might have done a very good job, there might have been a future public event planned which called for consistency in leadership (and in name), or a vacancy in the line of officers may have occurred which required the Master to serve again until others were ready to step up.

Five members have served as Master three different years, including Albert T. Van Horne, all instances occurring before 1900. This may have been due primarily to good leadership. In Van Horne's case, he was elected for the third time the year his centennial history was published.

Phinney himself served four times, the first three years of the lodge's existence and again in 1801. William Sprague also served four times in a similar pattern before the lodge was even twenty years old. Two men served as Master eight times, Charles Thurston and Eliab P. Byram, and Ariel Thayer served as Master an amazing fifteen times! Thayer and Thurston are easy to explain; they served during and immediately following the Morgan Period when the lodge went underground and met in secret only once per year. Thayer first served in 1825 and then again in 1856 after an eight-year absence. One can only wonder why.

E. P. Byram in an interesting case. His description of the lodge following the Morgan Period (quoted by Van Horne on page 23), while possibly self-promoting, is a little confusing. His statement infers that he knew of the dilapidated state of both the organization and its building *before* he became a Mason. Basically he claims to have single-handedly saved the lodge from going under, that being his sole purpose for joining. It is unclear why he would do that for an organization of which he was not a member, and which was at that time still considered suspect by many.

Frederick A. Goffe (five times) and Addison Gardner (seven times) are more of a mystery. They served during what seemed to be prosperous times for Otsego Lodge, when membership levels were relatively high. A guess, without scrutiny of the meeting minutes, leaves no other conclusion than internal lodge politics and power struggles between competing factions leading to their re-election. Such things do occur in any organization with that many members,.

Because of its existence for more than two centuries, the roster of Otsego Lodge Masters shows some identical surnames, evidence of multi-generational Freemasons in Cooperstown. The Dunn family, as mentioned elsewhere, has contributed three Masters to the lodge: Alton G. Dunn, Sr. (1933), Alton G. Dunn, Jr. (1958) and the current Master, Alton G. Dunn III (2006-2007). Other families have seen two generations serve as Master: Ellsworth, Spraker, Clark and Carso are just some of the fathers and sons who have held this distinction. A genealogical survey will surely add many more names to the list.

Whatever the case, just a quick perusal of the list reveals the names of community leaders whom many never knew were Freemasons. After just such an incident, a visitor to the lodge's recent Open House could only describe these men as "mighty." The qualities of leadership can be inherent in a person, but for many of these men, their leadership "training" came in the Masonic lodge as they worked their way up through the line of offices to sit in the honored chair as Worshipful Master of Otsego Lodge.

Year	Name	Year	Name
1796	Elihu Phinney	1818	William Nichols
1797	Elihu Phinney	1819	Ambrose L. Jordan
1798	Elihu Phinney	1820	Hervey Luce
1799	Richard Edwards	1821	E. B. Crandall
1800	Richard Edwards	1822	E. B. Crandall
1801	Elihu Phinney	1823	Hervey Luce
1802	Joshua Dewey	1824	E. B. Crandall
1803	Joshua Dewey	1825	Ariel Thayer
1804	Joshua Dewey	1826	E. B. Crandall
1805	E. H. Metcalf	1827	Ariel Thayer
1806	E. H. Metcalf	1828	Ariel Thayer
1807	E. H. Metcalf	1829	Ariel Thayer
1808	William Sprague	1830	Ariel Thayer
1809	William Sprague	1831	Ariel Thayer
1810	William Sprague	1832	Ariel Thayer
1811	Benjamin Wright	1833	Ariel Thayer
1812	Chester Griswold	1834	Ariel Thayer
1813	William Sprague	1835	Ariel Thayer
1814	Roger Haskell	1836	Charles Thurston
1815	Samuel Starkweather	1837	Charles Thurston
1816	Samuel Starkweather	1838	Joseph White
1817	William Nichols	1839	Ariel Thayer

Year	Name	Year	Name
1840	Charles Thurston	1884	Addison Gardner
1841	Charles Thurston	1885	Addison Gardner
1842	Charles Thurston	1886	Addison Gardner
1843	Charles Thurston	1887	Albert T. Van Horne
1844	Charles Thurston	1888	Albert T. Van Horne
1845	Charles Thurston	1889	Addison Gardner
1846	Ariel Thayer	1890	Andrew Davidson
1847	Ariel Thayer	1891	Addison Gardner
1848	Ariel Thayer	1892	Addison Gardner
1849	James Hyde	1893	George A. Hines
1850	James L. Fox	1894	William Cobbett
1851	James L. Fox	1895	William Cobbett
1852	James L. Fox	1896	Albert T. Van Horne
1853	Eliab P. Byram	1897	Nathaniel P. Willis
1854	Eliab P. Byram	1898	Nathaniel P. Willis
1855	Eliab P. Byram	1899	Frank Hale
1856	Ariel Thayer	1900	Frank Hale
1857	Eliab P. Byram	1901	Frank B. Shipman
1858	Eliab P. Byram	1902	Frank B. Shipman
1859	Eliab P. Byram	1903	Moses E. Lippitt
1860	Delos L. Birge	1904	Merton Barnes
1861	Eliab P. Byram	1905	George H. Carley
1862	Eliab P. Byram	1906	George W. Morris
1863	Rufus C. Doubleday	1907	Ernest L. Pitcher
1864	Charles W. Thomlinson	1908	Clarence W. Davidson
1865	Charles W. Thomlinson	1909	J. Ceylon Peaslee
1866	Charles W. Thomlinson	1910	Clarence W. Davidson
1867	James A. Lynes	1911	Frank M. Hotaling
1868	James A. Lynes	1912	Frank M. Hotaling
1869	Frederick A. Goffe	1913	Everett A. Rounds
1870	Frederick A. Goffe	1914	Ernest M. Clapsaddle
1871	Nelson Beach	1915	Willard C. Fowler
1872	Seth J. Temple	1916	Edward D. Lindsay
1873	Seth J. Temple	1917	Ralph W. Ellsworth
1874	Frederick A. Goffe	1918	Adrian A. Pierson
1875	Frederick A. Goffe	1919	Adrian A. Pierson
1876	Lyman H. Hills	1920	John L. Marshall
1877	Frederick A. Goffe	1921	John L. Marshall
1878	Washington G. Smith	1922	Rowan D. Spraker, Sr.
1879	James Bowes	1923	Harris L. Cooke
1880	James Bowes	1924	H. Harrington Yule
1881	Henry L. Hinman	1925	Alfred R. Cobbett
1882	Henry L. Hinman	1926	Harry J. Ballard
1883	Addison Gardner	1927	G. Reed Sill

Year	Name	Year	Name
1928	Frank C. Carpenter	1968	Clark F. Miller
1929	Fletcher A. Blanchard	1969	Pershing R. Dickinson
1930	Clyde S. Becker	1970	Robert C. Butler
1931	Ernest R. Lippitt	1971	Malcolm N. Brooks
1932	Andrew J. Gilchriest	1972	James E. Jackson
1933	Alton G. Dunn, Sr.	1973	Robert L. Ballard
1934	Bruce L. Hall	1974	Harold J. Saxton
1935	Carl H. Johnson	1975	Louis J. Bobnick
1936	J. Harry Cook	1976	Robert C. Butler
1937	Lester G. Bursey	1977	Harold L. Dodge
1938	Arthur J. Goddard	1978	Harry N. McManus
1939	Ralph W. Perry	1979	John F. Lettis
1940	Chester W. Ingalls	1980	Ronald F. Jex
1941	Robert M. Atwell	1981	Howard R. Sloan
1942	Bernard D. Carr	1982	Alfred J. Bleich
1943	Howard P. Michaels	1983	John A. Snyder
1944	Rowan D. Spraker, Jr.	1984	Charles Hadcock
1945	Gordon S. Winnie	1985	Harold F. Schneider
1946	Carl M. Green	1986	Helmut P. Bussmann
1947	Francis E. Clark	1987	Frank J. Kranitz
1948	Howard W. Potts	1988	Gerald B. Ellsworth
1949	George G. Tillapaugh	1989	William S. Griffith
1950	Oron W. Gage	1990	William T. Collins
1951	Harris G. Clark, Sr.	1991	William T. Collins
1952	Perry R. Hotaling	1992	Frank J. Kranitz
1953	Clifford L. Snyder	1993	Brian F. Carso, Sr.
1954	Harold H. Hollis	1994	Harris G. Clark, Jr.
1955	William N. Bliss	1995	Harris G. Clark, Jr.
1956	Charles D. Ellsworth	1996	Peter A. Deysenroth
1957	Harold J. Saxton	1997	William F. Cernik
1958	Alton G. Dunn, Jr.	1998	Dominick J. Reisen
1959	George H. Harrison	1999	Richard A. Vang
1960	Pershing R. Dickinson	2000	Brian F. Carso, Jr.
1961	Norman R. Peabody	2001	Mark W. MacLeod
1962	Charles C. Root	2002	Mark W. MacLeod
1963	Frank J. McKelvey	2003	Erik M. Strohl
1964	Clyde K. Ballard	2004	Christopher J. Barown
1965	Arthur Jenkins, Jr.	2005	Christopher J. Barown
1966	Kenneth M. Augur	2006	Alton G. Dunn III
1967	Robert J. Clark	2007	Alton G. Dunn III

Noteworthy Members of Otsego Lodge

Throughout its existence, Otsego Lodge has included many prominent Cooperstonians among its members, who have played an important role in the public life of the village, county and state. Familiar names like Augur, Lippitt, Davidson, Sill, Ellsworth, Cook, McEwan, Tillapaugh, Bruce Hall and George "Cap" Smith are listed in the lodge archives alongside more famous names like Stephen Clark and Erastus Beadle, the "Dime Novel King." These men joined in many public processions and helped to lay the cornerstones of many public buildings. Today's members contribute just as much to village life as their predecessors did, many of them in their own quiet way.

Interestingly, neither Judge Cooper nor his more famous son ever became Masons—an odd fact considering that many of their Albany and New York City friends were. The village founder did support the lodge in many ways despite his public quarrels with its members. He saw a Masonic lodge as a part of the apparatus of a prosperous town.

The following list of noteworthy lodge members is by no means exhaustive. The handful of names selected should be familiar to most residents of the village in one way or another, and should provide some interesting information. Further research would undoubtedly increase the list ten-fold.

Elihu Phinney

Elihu Phinney came to Cooperstown at the request of William Cooper to publish a newspaper. For many years he published *The Otsego Herald or Western Advertiser* as well as bibles and an almanac. He was the lead petitioner for the Otsego Lodge charter in 1795 and he became the first master of Otsego Lodge No. 40 in 1796. In addition to several papers and letters in the lodge archives, a portrait of Phinney hangs in the lodge room. It is a copy by John Lippitt, based on the original by fellow Mason Ezra Ames, held in the collection at the New York State Historical Association. (See portrait on page 80.)

General Jacob Morris

During the American Revolution Jacob Morris was an aide-de-camp to Generals Charles Lee and Nathaniel Greene, and was later commissioned a Major-General of the New York State militia. For their efforts towards American independence, his father Lewis (a signer of the Declaration) and uncle received lands along the Butternuts Creek in 1787. Jacob joined them there and became one of the major combatants of the early Otsego "political wars." He served as Supervisor of the Town of Butternuts, was the first Clerk of Otsego County, and was later elected to both the state Assembly and Senate. In 1796 he became one of the first initiates into the new Otsego Lodge No. 40 and later was the founder of the lodge in Butternuts. The Town of Morris was named in his honor.

Colonel Richard Cary
Richard Cary received his first two degrees in a military lodge during the American Revolution, but due to the instability and constant movement of the unit he was unable to achieve the third degree. When George Washington, an ardent Mason, toured the Otsego Lake area and visited Cary at his "Rose Lawn" estate (later "Swanswick"), he encouraged his former aid-de-camp to continue his Masonic journey. Finally, in 1796, Cary was raised to the degree of Master Mason in Otsego Lodge No. 40.

General Erastus Root
General Root was admitted to the bar in 1796 and set up practice in nearby Delhi. He became an affiliate member of the new Otsego Lodge No. 40 in Cooperstown that same year. Root was instrumental to the development of Delaware County and the State of New York. His list of accomplishments include being a member (as well as Speaker) of the state Assembly, a member of the state Senate, a delegate to the state constitutional convention, Lieutenant Governor, a Major-General of the state militia, and a member of the U.S. House of representatives. Root was a political nomad; he has been cataloged at various stages of his career as a Democrat, a Republican, a Jacksonian and a Whig.

Justice Samuel Nelson
Samuel Nelson moved to Cooperstown in 1826 because of his new bride's connection to the village. A respected attorney and a delegate to the state constitutional convention, Nelson soon became a Circuit Court Judge who, in 1831, became one of several that eventually presided over the prolonged trials of the Morgan affair. During his tenure he often brought the Circuit Court to his resort town where he spent his summers. In 1844 he became a Director of the Otsego County Bank (the first in Cooperstown), and the next year he was elevated to a seat on the U.S. Supreme Court as an Associate Justice. As the respected author of the majority opinion in *Dred Scott v. Sandford*, President Lincoln once sent his Secretary of State and other dignitaries to Cooperstown in 1863 to obtain Nelson's opinion on the constitutionality of the military draft. That same year he was instrumental in rebuilding the center of the village after a devastating fire. Nelson's

memory is perpetuated by a plaque on his former house on Main Street and by his grave site in Lakewood Cemetery.

Samuel Nelson is documented as being a member of Solomon's Lodge No. 5 in either Poughkeepsie or New York City, but that has been difficult to verify. To date, no evidence of his membership in Otsego Lodge has been found. His son Rensselaer was a member, so it is hard to imagine that a Mason who was so involved in a community (and which loved him in return) did not join the local lodge, or at the very least, visit a few times. He is included in this list of noteworthy lodge members until further research sheds more light on his membership.

Erastus Flavel Beadle

Erastus Beadle was born in Pierstown. At age 17 he became apprenticed to H. & E. Phinney, printers and binders. He stayed until 1847, learning much about typesetting, printing, stereotyping, binding and publishing. In 1851 Beadle published his first magazine for young children. Subsequent travels and failed business ventures in the American West gave him first-hand "knowledge" of the tales that would come to be synonymous with the name Beadle. Thousands of books and magazines were published over the decades, and "Beadle's Dime Novels" helped established pulp fiction firmly in American culture. In 1889, he retired to his summer home in Cooperstown. At the time of his death in 1894, he owned eight houses in the village. He was unique in the annals of Freemasonry, in that he did not complete his Fellowcraft (1890) and Master Mason (1891) degrees until he had retired to Cooperstown—forty-four years after he was initiated as an Entered Apprentice.

Stephen C. Clark, Sr.

Stephen Carlton Clark, Sr. was a capable heir to the Singer sewing fortune who later earned his reputation as a philanthropist, art collector and founder of museums such as the National Baseball Hall of Fame and Museum of Modern Art. Often away on business from the village that is synonymous with his name, he had to repeatedly reschedule each degree due to his duties as a member of the New York State Assembly. He was eventually raised to the degree of Master Mason in Cooperstown late in 1910.

John Harry Cook

J. Harry Cook was Master of Otsego Lodge No. 138 in 1936 and a local businessman of some note. In 1919 he bought out the last livery in Cooperstown and replaced it with an auto dealership. In 1928 he built the impressive brick building at 139 Main Street for his dealership and garage. As a member of Otsego Commandery No. 76, Knights Templar, Cook rose to the highest position in the Grand Commandery of New York. His installation as Right Eminent Grand Commander in 1952 saw one of the largest Masonic parades ever held in Cooperstown.

Howard W. Potts

The Masonic career of Howard Potts spanned several decades. For twenty-four years he served as the Grand Lecturer of the Grand Lodge of the State of New York. He was much beloved across the state for both his Masonic knowledge and his warm personality, as the numerous documents from lodges and districts in his personal papers attest. Today, the Grand Lodge presents the Howard Potts Award to each lodge that has complete attendance for its officers at their district's Grand Lecturer's Convention. Otsego Lodge received the Potts Award in 2003.

Gerald B. Ellsworth

A second generation Master of Otsego Lodge, Gerald Ellsworth was the epitome of community service. Following his premature death at age 54, it was estimated that it took eight people to fill his many public and philanthropic positions. Among his roles were: member of the school board, alumni association president, village library trustee, hospital volunteer, village walking tour guide, high school theater director, Scout master, local newspaper columnist and—probably one of his most beloved roles—portraying Santa Claus for the village's children at Christmas.

Sources

While these sources have been consulted from time to time over the years, they are presented here not as bibliographic references for this book, but rather as suggested sources for further reading and information. Those not familiar with Freemasonry will find some sources useful; others will find the information about Cooperstown more to their liking.

William Cooper's Town: Power and Persuasion on the Frontier of the Early American Republic by Alan Taylor is an excellent book on the founding period of the village and the development of the surrounding area in general. Cooperstown by Louis C. Jones provides a good overview of the village and its more important organizations and influences.

Those readers wanting to learn more about Freemasonry in general should consult The Complete Idiot's Guide to Freemasonry by S. Brent Morris. Two good sources for the history of Masonry in New York State are Masonic Trails of Early New York, a collection of essays by Wilmer Bresee (published in Vol. XV, No. 1 of the *Transactions of the American Lodge of Research*) and Ossian Lang's History of Freemasonry in the State of New York (published by the Grand Lodge of New York). All three of these books are useful to the Mason who wants to increase his knowledge of Freemasonry.

For another source of information and visual images, readers should visit the web site of The Chancellor Robert R Livingston Masonic Library of Grand Lodge at *http://www.nymasoniclibrary.org*. Supported by the Grand Lodge of Free and Accepted Masons of the State of New York, the Livingston Library is celebrating 150 years as the premier Masonic library. The web site features a virtual museum of important artifacts, photos and biographies of important New York Freemasons, and an online book catalogue.

About the Editor

Richard Vang is a Past Master, Past Trustee, and the current Historian of Otsego Lodge. He serves as a Trustee of The Chancellor Robert R Livingston Masonic Library of Grand Lodge (NY), and is a member of the Scottish Rite Valleys of Schenectady (NY) and Santa Fe (NM), the Santa Fe York Rite Bodies, and The Philalethes Society. A former Trustee of the Cooperstown Village Library, he holds a B.A. in Literature and Folklore from Binghamton University. The author of numerous articles over the past 15 years, his most recent work is the children's book, My Dad is a Freemason. He and his family live in the Helderberg Mountains near Albany, New York.

How to Order

To order copies of this book, please visit our web site at:

www.squarecirclepress.com

A portion of the proceeds derived from the sale of this book is donated to Otsego Lodge No. 138 for charitable purposes and to preserve items of historical significance to the lodge.

Square Circle Press

www.ingramcontent.com/pod-product-compliance
Lightning Source LLC
Chambersburg PA
CBHW021020090426
42738CB00007B/836